C000021033

The Primary Teacher's Guide to

Phonics

• Key subject knowledge • Background information • Teaching tips •

Wendy Jolliffe

◼SCHOLASTIC

Book End, Range Road, Witney, Oxfordshire,
OX29 0YD

www.scholastic.co.uk

© 2013 Scholastic Ltd

1 2 3 4 5 6 7 8 9   3 4 5 6 7 8 9 0 1 2

British Library Cataloguing-in-Publication Data
A catalogue record for this book is available from the
British Library.

ISBN 978-1407-12796-5

Printed and bound by CPI Group (UK) Ltd, Croydon,
CR0 4YY

Author
Wendy Jolliffe

Editorial team
Rachel Morgan, Melissa Rugless,
Tracy Kewley, Suzanne Adams

Indexer
Sue Lightfoot

Icons
Tomek.gr

Series Designers
Shelley Best and Sarah Garbett

Acknowledgements

The publishers gratefully acknowledge permission
to reproduce the following copyright material:

Jan G. Nolst Trenité Foundation for the use
of the poem 'The Chaos' by G. Nolst Trenité
from Drop Your Foreign Accent - Engelse
Uitspraakoefeningen by G. Nolst Trenite. Poem ©
1922, G. Nolst Trenité (1922, H. D. Tjeenk Willink
& Zoon).

Every effort has been made to trace copyright
holders for the works reproduced in this book,
and the publishers apologise for any inadvertent
omissions.

Contents

Icon key

Information within this book is highlighted in the margins by a series of different icons. They are:

Subject facts
Key subject knowledge is clearly presented and explained in this section.

Why you need to know these facts
Provides justification for understanding the facts that have been explained in the previous section.

Vocabulary
A list of key words, terms and language relevant to the preceding section. Vocabulary entries appear in the glossary.

Amazing facts
Interesting snippets of background knowledge to share.

Common misconceptions
Identifies and corrects some of the common misconceptions and beliefs that may be held about the subject area.

Questions
Identifies common questions and provides advice on how to answer them.

Handy tips
Specific tips or guidance on best practice in the classroom.

Teaching ideas
Outlines practical teaching suggestions using the knowledgeexplained in the preceding section.

Phonics

This book aims to provide an overview of the role of phonics in the teaching of reading, and how to crack the alphabetic code in English. Learning to read and write is far more complex in English than in many other languages as the English language has evolved over centuries, with many cultural influences. This has resulted in a lack of transparency between the letters and sounds of the language, meaning there is no direct correspondence between the (approximately) 44 phonemes or sounds and the 26 letters that represent them.

This book explains the phonetic structure of the language and is interspersed with teaching ideas and handy tips to help break down these structures into easily understandable chunks to support the teaching of reading to young children.

Government commitment to phonics

The issue of phonics continues to produce much debate, not just in academic journals but also in the media. While the debate will doubtless continue, governments in the UK and elsewhere in the English-speaking world have made a firm commitment to support the teaching of phonics, based on extensive reviews of the research. In the UK, this is likely to be made statutory in the new National Curriculum for 2014. The draft curriculum states:

> *Skilled word reading involves both the speedy working out of the pronunciation of unfamiliar printed words (decoding) and the speedy recognition of familiar printed words. Underpinning both is the understanding that the letters on the page represent the sounds in spoken words. This is why phonics should be emphasised in the early teaching of reading to beginners (i.e. unskilled readers) when they start school.*
> *(National Curriculum for English Key Stages 1 and 2 – Draft, DfE, 2012)*

Subject knowledge

Teachers and those training to teach need to have an in-depth understanding of phonics and how to teach it effectively. For many who have not studied linguistics before, this is a whole new body of knowledge and can cause real concerns. However, once a clear understanding is provided of the phonic structure of the language and how this can be taught even to young children, these anxieties disappear. To become proficient, of course, application in practice, with feedback from an expert, is required.

One of the key aims of this book is to support subject knowledge for teaching so it is useful to consider the meaning of the term 'subject knowledge'. The Training and Development Agency (TDA) in 2007 set out a useful framework for looking at subject knowledge, as follows:

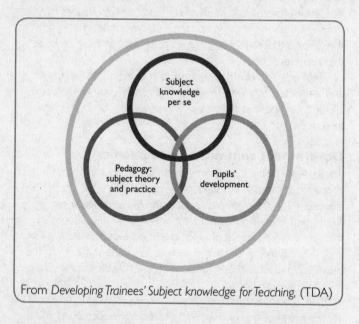

From *Developing Trainees' Subject knowledge for Teaching.* (TDA)

'Subject knowledge per se' refers to the essential knowledge and understanding needed in order to teach a subject effectively. 'Pedagogy: subject theory and practice' refers to the range of teaching skills and strategies that a teacher can use to promote children's learning in the subject. It is also crucial to consider children's development: how children's learning in the subject is affected by developmental, social, religious, ethnic, cultural and linguistic influences. Another important aspect concerns children's attitudes: the need for children to have the positive attitudes to learning that underpin subject knowledge, skills and understanding. This book looks specifically at subject knowledge and pedagogy, and while it does not include discussion about children's development and attitudes, these factors need to be carefully considered in any application in practice.

What does this book cover?

The book begins by looking at the place of phonics in the teaching of reading and shows how phonics supports word recognition – one aspect of becoming an efficient reader, alongside developing good language comprehension.

Chapter 2 examines phonological awareness – the ability to perceive, recall and manipulate sounds – and explains how to support this, including guidance on when to provide additional phonological awareness training.

Chapter 3 examines the alphabetic code, or principle, which refers to the understanding that letters are used to represent the speech sounds of our language. The concepts that underpin this and how this can be taught effectively are explored in depth, including the key differences between the basic and the complex alphabetic code. How to enunciate the phonemes correctly, and why this is important in phonics teaching, is also explored in this chapter. Common difficulties, such as accent and the use of letter names as well as sounds, are also discussed.

In Chapter 4 the most complex aspect of teaching phonics is dealt with: the long-vowel phonemes and how these can be taught, even to young children, using multi-sensory methods.

Chapter 5 considers the application of phonics in reading and writing, which is one of the keys to successfully learning phonics. How encoding (spelling) and decoding (reading) can be frequently applied in every lesson is reviewed, together with the role of segmenting and blending.

Chapter 6 looks at 'common exception words': words that are some of the most common in English usage but that are not easily decodable. The derivation of these words and how these can be taught, at least in part, as whole words is also addressed.

Chapter 7 considers a systematic progression for teaching phonics that ensures all 44 phonemes and their major spellings are taught in a clear sequence. It also looks at some of the well-known phonics programmes and how these are structured.

Chapter 8 concludes the book with a detailed review of how to assess children's learning in phonics. It explains how one of the most important aspects of teaching phonics effectively is the accurate tracking and ongoing review of children's progress to support diagnostic assessment of specific children's needs. This chapter also explores the phonics screening test introduced by the Government in 2012, which can be used by teachers to support diagnostic assessment.

It is hoped the book will offer clear guidance to support effective subject knowledge for teaching phonics and be a useful reference book for both experienced and trainee teachers.

Phonics and reading

Debates have raged over phonics as the key method to teaching reading. Governments in the UK, the USA and elsewhere have placed a high level of importance on phonics. In England this has culminated in a focus on phonics in inspections of schools by Ofsted, in initial teacher training and, in 2012, the introduction of the phonics screening check for six-year-olds. In the context of media 'hype' and Government pressure, it becomes increasingly important to have a clear understanding of what phonics contributes to the teaching of reading and writing. This chapter summarises the role of phonics.

What's involved in learning to read?

Subject facts

One analogy used for phonics and decoding skills is that of a car. A car needs fuel as a pre-requisite for it to go but, in order to function, it requires the many parts of the car engine to work. Decoding can be likened to the fuel: you can't read if you can't decipher the marks on the page, but deciphering the marks, or letters, into words is not the whole story – just like a car which needs more than fuel to drive along the road. Read this example:

> Hence if the import of the judgement of taste, where we appraise it as a judgement entitled to require the concurrence of every one, cannot be egoistic, but must necessarily, from its inner nature, be allowed a pluralistic validity, i.e. on account of what itself is, then it must be founded upon some a priori principle

(be it subjective or objective) and no amount of prying into the empirical laws of the changes that go on within the mind can succeed in establishing such a principle.

Critique of Judgement by Immanuel Kant

Unless you understand such philosophical concepts, reading these words is meaningless. You can probably decipher the words, but have no idea what you are reading. In other words, reading requires two key activities: firstly, decoding or word recognition; and secondly understanding, so that individual words become meaningful sentences within a familiar context.

The simple view of reading

The two key aspects 'word recognition' and 'language comprehension' have been combined in a model called the 'simple view of reading' (Gough and Tunmer, 1986) which has been widely recommended by the Government, in particular since the Rose Review of the teaching of reading in 2006. This model of reading is represented in the diagram below.

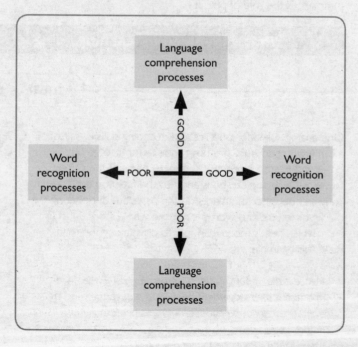

The role of phonics

So how does phonics fit into this model? Phonics supports the decoding of words, or as described in the simple view of reading, 'word recognition'. For example, to read the word 'tap' using phonics you need to recognise each letter, say the sound it represents and then blend the sounds into a word: /t/ /a/ /p/ = *tap*. Another way of reading a word is to learn the visual representation of the whole word. This was commonly used as a reading method in the past and was termed 'look and say'. The problem with this, however, is that it relies on a good visual memory and provides no strategies for decoding unfamiliar or more complex words. Teaching phonics early and systematically is, therefore, crucially important as it provides children with a strategy for decoding words as they encounter them. It also supports children's spelling (encoding) skills.

The complexity of English

The English language, however, presents a problem when applying phonics. Unlike other languages, such as Finnish or Italian, it is not phonically regular and one letter does not always make one sound. This has been regarded as a major stumbling block to teaching phonics in the past. Even in common words the use of phonics can be problematic. For example, when a word such as *was* is sounded out – /w/ /a/ /s/ – it does not appear to make the word 'was'. Accordingly, young children often write the word as 'woz', demonstrating that the correspondence between the sounds and the words is not always transparent in English. This is one example of a high-frequency 'common exception' word, which chapter 6 explores in depth, with suggestions of how to overcome such problems. But these inconsistencies do not mean that phonics doesn't work. There are over 170 common patterns in our words in English and learning phonics provides an important insight into these patterns.

To summarise, teaching phonics effectively, in a systematic progression, supports children in developing the key skills to read and also to write. On its own, phonics will not develop efficient readers: to do that requires the skills of language comprehension. However, phonics is a crucial part, acting as the fuel in the engine of reading.

Why you need to know these facts

- A lack of understanding of the role of phonics in learning to read and to write could mean that teachers and parents think that the use of phonics is all that is required. Without developing comprehension skills, children will not learn to read effectively; although you could use decoding skills to read the words in the extract from Kant, this would not mean that you would understand the extract's meaning. What is the point of reading without understanding?

- The phonic structure or alphabetic code in English is complex: a letter does not always make the same sound and sometimes it is a combination of letters that make one sound. In spite of this complexity, phonics provides a strategy for decoding words, whether we have encountered them before or not, and supports children to spell words more effectively. Chapter 3 examines the alphabetic code in detail.

Vocabulary

Decoding – the act of translating graphemes, or letters, into phonemes, or sounds, in order to read words.
Encoding – the act of transcribing units of sound, or phonemes, into graphemes for spelling words.
Language comprehension – the process by which words, sentences and discourse are interpreted.
Word recognition – the ability to recognise words out of context and to apply phonic rules to this recognition.

Amazing facts

Reading is a highly complex process that requires the brain to undertake a number of functions. This includes the recognition of letters and their combinations (the orthographic process);

the ability to translate those letters into corresponding sounds (the phonological process), and then to create meaning from the words and sentences (the semantic process).

As we read sentences, we process the words and their related meanings into coherent sequences, which makes considerable demands on our memory and on our speed of processing. In order to understand more complex text, we need to make use of our knowledge of the context and make deductions from clues in the text. Below is a list of the processes that research (by William Grabe and Fredricka Stoller) has shown occur every two seconds in our reading.

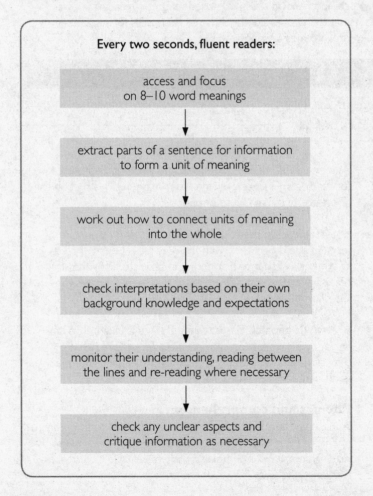

Every two seconds, fluent readers:

access and focus on 8–10 word meanings

↓

extract parts of a sentence for information to form a unit of meaning

↓

work out how to connect units of meaning into the whole

↓

check interpretations based on their own background knowledge and expectations

↓

monitor their understanding, reading between the lines and re-reading where necessary

↓

check any unclear aspects and critique information as necessary

What the graphic shows is that reading is a highly complex process and that the more automatic some parts can be, such as the decoding of the words, and the more quickly the whole process can be achieved, the better.

Common misconceptions

It is a misconception that those who advocate the importance of teaching phonics do this at the expense of teaching language comprehension skills. Any skilled teacher of reading knows that the two go side by side. See Resources for suggested programmes to support his.

Types of phonics

Subject facts

As much as the debate rages over the teaching methods used for reading, so it does over the types of phonics instruction used. There are two main types of phonics:

● **Systematic synthetic phonics:** This is phonics taught in a systematic progression with the core aspect being the use of synthesis of sounds or blending in order to apply the skill to reading words and the reversible skill of segmenting words into their constituent sounds.

● **Analytic phonics:** This is where phonics is taught through analogy with words, for example if children can read *man*, they can also read *pan*, *fan* and *can* by substituting different initial consonants or consonant blends.

Phonics and comprehension
A third type of phonics teaching is often referred to as 'contextual phonics'. This is where phonics instruction is integrated with reading-comprehension training, using meaningful experiences with engaging texts. However, it is unclear why any phonics

teaching could not be included within a programme that also seeks to develop language comprehension, thus promoting both main aspects of the simple view of reading at the same time. Some suggested teaching ideas for ensuring that word recognition and comprehension skills are developed in tandem are provided below.

The current approach

The approach currently recommended by the UK Government is systematic synthetic phonics, and this is backed up by two large international reports, in addition to the Rose Review: *Teaching Children to Read*, the report of the National Reading Panel in the USA in 2000, and *Teaching Reading*, the Australian Government review of 2005. Advantages cited for this approach:

- It ensures a systematic progression where all the major letter/sound correspondences (grapheme/phoneme correspondences or GPCs) are taught fast and early, enabling children to apply them in their reading and writing.
- It provides opportunities for all children to make progress without a need to rely on skills such as visual memory.
- It can and should be embedded within a broad and language-rich curriculum.
- It can be taught in lively interactive ways using multi-sensory teaching methods.
- It has been shown to produce superior results in a range of research studies.
- As English is more complex than many languages, a systematic approach to teaching the alphabetic code is beneficial, as stated in the Rose Review: *It cannot be left to chance, or for children to ferret out, on their own, how the alphabetic code works.*

Why you need to know these facts

● Having a clear understanding of the different types of phonics will ensure that these are used appropriately. It will also ensure that teaching is based on a clear understanding of why certain approaches should be used, and what evidence there is for their effectiveness.

Vocabulary

Analytic phonics – an approach to the teaching of reading in which the phonemes associated with particular graphemes are not pronounced in isolation. Children identify (analyse) the common phonemes in a set of words that each contain the phonemes under study, for example *could, would, should; can, pan, man*. Analytic phonics for writing similarly relies on inferential learning. This approach is often linked to the use of 'Onset' and 'Rime'.

Grapheme – a written representation of a phoneme, that is, a letter or group of letters representing a sound. There is always the same number of graphemes in a word as phonemes. The alphabet contains only 26 letters, but by combining the letters in different combinations we can form all the graphemes that represent the phonemes of English.

Grapheme/phoneme correspondence (GPC) – the relationship between the letters and the sounds they represent.

Onset – in analytic phonics, this is the first part of a word: the consonant or adjacent consonants at the beginning and before the vowel, for example 'fl-' in *flat*.

Phoneme – the smallest unit of sound in a word that can change its meaning (for example, the difference between the phonemes /b/ and /l/ signals the difference in meaning between the words *bed* and *led*). It is generally accepted that most varieties of spoken English use about 44 phonemes. In alphabetic writing systems (such as English) phonemes are represented by graphemes.

Rime – in analytic phonics, this is the final part of the word: the vowel sound and any consonant sounds that follow it, for example '-at' in *flat*.

Synthetic phonics – an approach to the teaching of reading in which the phonemes (sounds) associated with particular graphemes (letters) are pronounced in isolation and blended together (synthesised). Synthetic phonics for writing reverses the sequence: children are taught to say the word they wish to write, segment it into its phonemes and say them in turn, and write a grapheme for each phoneme in turn to produce the written word.

Common misconceptions

The term 'synthetic phonics' is often seen as suggesting something artificial and can thus be interpreted as derogatory. In fact synthetic phonics refers to the process of synthesising sounds or phonemes. Learning to sound out the letters and combinations is not enough – they have to be synthesised together to make words. Simply saying a list of sounds one after the other, for example /f/ /l/ /a/ /t/, is no use at all unless they can be blended together to make a whole word *flat*. This skill of blending needs to be explicitly taught and this is a key part of synthetic phonics, together with the reversible process of segmenting a word into its constituent phonemes, the skill required to spell the word.

Teaching ideas

Some of the key points in putting systematic synthetic phonics into practice within an effective reading programme are given below.

Beginning readers

In addition to providing a broad and rich language curriculum, including a varied diet of books to be explored in interactive ways, ensure there are opportunities for children to develop in the following areas:

● **Learning about print:** Use Big Books/enlarged texts to demonstrate how print works – from left to right and back to left, and from top to bottom of the page. Encourage children to identify individual letters, the spacing in between words and the punctuation used, and then aim to develop their understanding of the concept of a sentence.

● **Phonological awareness:** To help children develop good listening skills, begin with a focus on discriminating a range of sounds around them by listening to different sounds in the environment and playing games that help them to distinguish different sounds. You can then move on to larger 'units' of sound, exploring syllables and rhymes, with lots of activities involving listening to and playing with nursery rhymes or songs. Tapping out syllable patterns using a range of instruments can also enhance aural discrimination of syllables in words. This can then progress to exploring smaller 'units' of sound and distinguishing individual phonemes, supported by a phonics programme.

● **Alphabet awareness:** Children should be introduced to the alphabet using letter names, for example by using alphabet songs and rhymes. Knowledge of letter names should not be confused with learning phonemes.

● **Vocabulary:** Begin to develop children's vocabulary through introducing and explaining words outside their experience as well as giving indirect instruction through providing a rich literary environment.

Learning to decode

While continuing to ensure a rich language curriculum, begin systematic phonics teaching, based on an assessment of children's needs.

● Provide systematic instruction in sound/symbol correspondences (decoding), ensuring that the complete alphabetic code is taught.

● Provide opportunities for children to hear, say, read and write the phonemes taught with plenty of practice and over-learning.

● Ensure that regular diagnostic assessment is undertaken to track children's progress, and intervene with additional support where required.

● Continue with explicit teaching of vocabulary.

Independent reading

During this stage the child moves from relying on decoding
to recognising an increasing number of words automatically.
The emphasis shifts to improving comprehension.

● Ensure that phonemic knowledge is secure and applied
in spelling through systematic teaching of spelling.

● Ensure that comprehension is developed at different levels
through shared, guided and independent reading, including:
- literal understanding of the text
- inferential or deductive understanding by reading between
  the lines and through paired and group discussion
- evaluative understanding of the text by comparing with
  other similar texts and identifying specific strengths.

Resources

Evidence-based reading reports:

Independent Review of the Teaching of Early Reading by Jim Rose
(DfES, 2006).
*Teaching Children to Read: An Evidence-Based Assessment of the
Scientific Research Literature on Reading and its Implications for
Reading Instruction* (National Reading Panel, USA, 2000)
Teaching Reading: National Inquiry into the Teaching of Literacy
(Department of Education, Science and Training, Australia,
2005)

Articles and books on reading theory and pedagogy:

'Decoding, reading and reading disability' by Philip Gough and
William Tunmer (*Remedial and Special Education*, 1986)
Teaching and Researching: Reading by William Grabe and Fredricka
Stoller (Pearson)
English 5–11: A Guide for Teachers by David Waugh and Wendy
Jolliffe (Routledge)

Phonological awareness

Phonological awareness is an umbrella term which refers to the ability to perceive, recall and manipulate sounds. It is the foundation of learning phonics, as children need to be able to hear and discriminate a range of sounds before learning to work with individual phonemes in words.

Phonological awareness is often confused with phonemic awareness. The latter relates to the ability to hear and manipulate the phonemes in spoken words and to remember the order of such phonemes. An example would be to ask a child to tell you the phonemes in the word *cat*: /c/ /a/ /t/. You might go on to work on changing a phoneme in the word, for example substituting /m/ for /c/ to make the word *mat*.

Developing phonological awareness

Subject facts

Teaching phonological awareness

In the past there was an emphasis on teaching phonological awareness prior to beginning teaching phonics. This was because it was felt that this was a skill that needed extensive training to be fully developed. More recent research shows us that while we need to ensure children have developed the skills of hearing and playing with sounds, lengthy teaching of this is not necessary for the majority of children. Most children, particularly those who have had rich experiences of playing with sounds and rhymes, continue to develop their phonological awareness alongside good teaching of grapheme/phoneme correspondences. Accurate assessment of their developing skills is important, therefore, and this will be discussed further in Chapter 8.

Additional phonological awareness training

Some children, however, may require additional support to develop good phonological awareness. This may be due to a range of factors, one of which could be problems with hearing. Many young children suffer from a condition known as 'glue ear' and this has an impact on their ability to develop phonological awareness. If you have concerns about a child's hearing, it is important to refer them to a medical practitioner who can assess them.

Studies of children at risk of delayed reading or reading failure (by Hatcher et al. 2004) found that combining rhyme with a reading programme was particularly effective. This included a structured programme of rhyme and phoneme awareness linked to the reading of text which included the same phonemes or rhymes. It specifically included the following sequence:

- Identification of words as units within sentences
- Identification and manipulation of syllables
- Discrimination of rhyming words
- Phoneme blending
- Identification and discrimination of phonemes
- Rhyme correction and supply
- Phoneme segmentation
- Phoneme deletion
- Phoneme substitution
- Phoneme transposition

Ways to develop phonological awareness

Although it is not necessary for most children to have extensive phonological awareness training, it is still important to develop these skills. Parents and teachers can enhance children's ability to discriminate and play with sounds in the following key ways:

● **Listening:** The first essential step in phonological awareness training is to ensure that children develop the skills of listening attentively before they try to discriminate fine differences in sounds. Alongside this is children's developing auditory recall, for example can they remember a sequence of sounds?

- **Rhyming:** Next, rhyming work needs to be taught, again in steps, starting with rhyme exposure (provide lots of opportunities for children to hear rhymes), then encouraging rhyme detection (ask children to identify whether words sound the same or different), and finally rhyme generation (children come up with their own rhymes).

- **Identifying words:** Another step in developing phonological awareness is ensuring that children can identify individual words from the continuous stream of speech that they hear.

- **Syllables:** Once the children can identify individual words, it is important to ensure that they can begin the process of breaking down words, first into syllables, before going on to break words into individual phonemes.

Why you need to know these facts

- It is important to understand how phonological awareness supports learning phonics and that, for most children, this is developed alongside rich literary experiences, including a developing knowledge of rhymes and nursery rhymes, together with systematic phonics teaching. Some children, however, do require specific phonological awareness training so it is key that all children are assessed so that any specific needs can be identified.

Vocabulary

Phonemic awareness – the ability to perceive and manipulate the phonemes in spoken words.
Phonological awareness – the ability to perceive, recall and manipulate sounds.

Amazing facts

Studies of language development demonstrate that awareness of phonemes is present at birth and, by about six months, children begin to extract words from the stream of speech they hear. Babies' early babbling demonstrates this too, with babies around the world all saying consonant/vowel sounds such as 'ba-da'. By three years of age, children are generally capable of demonstrating what they know and one study by Carolyn Chaney (1993) found that 93 per cent of three-year-olds could listen to a sequence of phonemes and blend them into a word.

Common misconceptions

The most common misconception is that young children are not able to discriminate sounds and phonemes without specific training. However, as described above, even young babies can begin to discriminate sounds.

A further misconception is that phonemic awareness and phonological awareness are the same. As discussed earlier, phonological awareness is the umbrella term for the ability to perceive, recall and manipulate sounds, while phonemic awareness refers purely to discriminating and manipulating phonemes in words.

Handy tip

In order to demonstrate how many syllables there are in a word, one strategy that is useful for children is to place your hand flat horizontally beneath your chin and say a word. The number of times your chin drops (equivalent to the number of vowel phonemes in the word) denotes the number of syllables (for example, *te-le-vi-sion* – four syllables).

Teaching ideas

Differentiation of sounds in the environment

● Collect a range of recorded sounds, such as the washing machine spinning, an alarm clock going off, a phone ringing, a car starting, or birds singing. Use these for various activities including playing sounds 'lotto' (matching corresponding pictures to the sounds heard), and making up stories that incorporate the sounds on the recording.

● Use musical instruments to help children discriminate volume and pitch. These could accompany a story read to children.

● Incorporate sounds into play activities, for example small-world toys such as farm animals and zoo animals can be used in conjunction with making the animal noises. An alternative could be to set up a role-play area that would naturally include plenty of different noises, such as a supermarket or a railway station.

Distinguishing individual words

● Read poems that repeat the same word often and ask children to carry out an action, such as touching their ear, every time they hear that specific word. A good example of a poem for this is 'A Busy Day' by Michael Rosen, which continually repeats the word 'pop'.

● Have fun with creating alliterative sentences, then say them emphasising each individual word, such as *Harry is happy, Wendy is wobbly, Ben is bumpy* and so on.

● Enjoy tongue-twisters such as 'Betty Botter':

Betty Botter bought some butter,
but, she said, the butter's bitter;
if I put it in my batter
it will make my batter bitter,
but a bit of better butter
will make by batter better.
So she bought a bit of butter

better than her bitter butter,
and she put it in her batter
and the batter was not bitter.
So 'twas better Betty Botter
bought a bit of better butter.

Knowledge of rhymes

● Play games such as 'spot the rhyme' with familiar nursery rhymes. The adult says the rhyme but pauses for the child to provide a rhyming word.

● Have fun with alternative rhymes, for example *Humpty Dumpty sat on a log, Humpty Dumpty saw a frog.* For a range of fun examples see *Nonsense Nursery Rhymes* by Richard Edwards and Chris Fisher (Oxford University Press).

● Read together a rhyming story such as *Each Peach Pear Plum* by Janet and Alan Ahlberg (Puffin) and stop before rhyming words, asking the children to supply them.

● Have a range of rhyming sentences available and ask the children to suggest the missing words, for example: *I went to bed and bumped my…. The shed was painted….*

● Collect a number of pictures of objects that rhyme for children to play pairs games with.

Differentiating syllables

● Play 'my turn, your turn' where you clap or beat the syllables in words and the children copy you.

● Regularly include opportunities for beating/tapping of names, with children taking turns. Musical instruments can be incorporated, for example a drum could be passed around the children for them to tap their name on. Have fun tapping patterns of names yourself (such as 'Har-ry Pot-ter') and ask children to guess whose name you are tapping.

● Using musical instruments, maintain a syllable pattern. Give a group of children instruments, such a xylophones, drums and so on, and ask them to repeat the pattern you make, at the same time as you say a string of words, such as *bread and butter, fish and chips, sausage and mash* and so on.

● Share a number of objects you have in a box. Ask a child to choose an object, but not to tell you or the other children which one. The child then claps the corresponding number of syllables and everyone has to guess what it is.

Teaching phonological awareness alongside a systematic phonics programme

Subject facts

A number of research studies (David Share, 1995, and Anne Castles and Max Coltheart, 2004) have demonstrated that combining training in phonological awareness with the teaching of reading-related skills such as grapheme/phoneme correspondences produces increased reading attainment. The key is teaching both together, as phonological awareness and alphabetic knowledge have a reciprocal relationship. Studies have also shown that phoneme awareness develops at the same time as children learn to read words. That is, children who read well also have good phonemic awareness. It is therefore necessary to first assess children's phonological awareness (see Resources for support in doing this), then to provide a training in distinguishing larger to smaller units of sounds (from words to phonemes). This should be carried out alongside systematic teaching of the correspondence between the 26 letters of English and the 44 (or more) phonemes. For guidance on systematic teaching of grapheme/phoneme correspondences, see Chapter 7.

Adults' phonemic awareness

For adults, phonemic awareness is at an unconscious level. They focus on the meaning and are not aware of individual phonemes in words. One common problem for adults is that they use their knowledge of the letters in the written word and this visual spelling pattern dominates when they try and segment words into the number of corresponding phonemes.

This is clearly demonstrated by asking a group of adults to say how many sounds are in a word such as *splash*. You will find that an assortment of numbers will be given. The common use of consonant clusters at the beginning of words causes confusion so that 'spl' is sometimes perceived to be one phoneme – when in fact it is a blend of three different phonemes. The word *splash* has five phonemes: /s/ /p/ /l/ /a/ /sh/. These factors – a focus on how a word is spelled and the common use of consonant blends in English words – leads to difficulties for adults in identifying the number of phonemes in a word. However, a clear understanding of the issues and plenty of practice in segmenting words can soon remedy this.

Vocabulary and phonological awareness

There is a link between children's vocabulary and their phonological awareness because, as vocabulary grows, there is pressure on the memory to store a greater number of phonological representations of words. Research suggests that gradually there is a restructuring of phonological representations of words from 'wholes' to 'segments', or phonemes.
This developing ability to store and recall, first the sounds of words and then, later, smaller units or phonemes, all supports the ultimate goal of reading: constructing meaning.

Why you need to know these facts

• Having a clear understanding of what phonological awareness is and how to promote it is a key aspect of teaching phonics. It is also important to note that extensive training is not needed for most children, as they develop this awareness alongside their learning of grapheme/phoneme correspondences. These skills are enhanced by developing children's language skills generally and, in particular, by promoting their knowledge of vocabulary.

Vocabulary

Blend – to draw sounds, or phonemes, together to pronounce a word, so /s/ /l/ /i/ /p/ equals *slip*.

Consonant cluster – two or more consonants that are commonly found at the beginning of words and that do not have an intervening vowel, for example 'str' in *stream*. These are also termed 'adjacent consonants'.

Segment – to split up a word into its constituent sounds, or phonemes, in order to spell it.

Questions

What are the key differences between phonological awareness and phonemic awareness?

Phonological awareness is the broad term which covers the ability to discriminate sounds generally. Phonemic awareness relates solely to the ability to hear and manipulate the phonemes in spoken words.

What activities support the development of phonological awareness?

Phonological awareness is supported through children developing good listening skills; exploring rhymes and generating their own; learning to detect individual words and hear alliteration in words; refining their skills so that they can discriminate syllables in words and then identify individual phonemes in words.

When is it necessary to provide additional phonological awareness training?

Additional phonological awareness training is necessary where children are identified as not clearly being able to discriminate between different sounds. For most children this ability develops alongside systematic phonics learning, because phonological awareness and alphabetic knowledge have a reciprocal relationship.

Teaching ideas

As Chapter 1 outlined, phonics is only one aspect in teaching reading. Any phonics programme should be taught within the context of a rich diet of language experiences. Phonological awareness is supported by these language experiences, and generally encouraging children to have a love of words and stories is also powerful in developing this awareness. Some ways of increasing their enjoyment include:

● Making use of children's literature in engaging ways. *We're Going on a Bear Hunt* by Michael Rosen (Walker Books) uses wonderful alliterative language (for example *swishy, swashy*) and repetition with which children can join in (chanting *We're not scared!*, perhaps getting louder when the text gets larger). You could also get them to act out the tiptoeing and so on, as they join in with the words.

● Using rhyming texts such as *Hairy Maclary from Donaldson's Dairy* by Lynley Dodd (Puffin), *Each Peach Pear Plum* and *The Jolly Postman* by Janet and Allan Ahlberg (Puffin), to name but a few.

● Playing with words and language, for example by enjoying poems and making up alternative lines such as *The Grand old Duke of York, who used a great big fork.*

Resources

Supporting development of phonological awareness

Nonsense Nursery Rhymes by Richard Edwards and Chris Fisher (Oxford University Press)
We're Going on a Bear Hunt by Michael Rosen (Walker)
Hairy Maclary from Donaldson's Dairy by Lynley Dodd (Puffin)
Books by Julia Donaldson, for example, *The Gruffalo*, *Room on the Broom* (Macmillan)
Books by Janet and Allan Ahlberg, for example *Each Peach Pear Plum*, *The Jolly Postman* (Puffin)
Books by Jez Alborough, for example, *Some Dogs Do* (Walker), *Duck in the Truck* (HarperCollins)

For assessment of children's phonological awareness

Quick Fix for Phonics by Wendy Jolliffe (Scholastic)

For more in-depth discussion of research in this area

Teaching Systematic Synthetic Phonics in Primary Schools by Wendy
    Jolliffe and David Waugh with Angela Carss (Sage)
'Explicit phoneme training combined with phonic reading
    instruction helps young children at risk of reading failure'
    by PJ Hatcher, C Hulme and MJ Snowling, (*Journal of Child
    Psychology and Psychiatry*, 2004)
'Language development, metalinguistic skills, and print
    awareness in 3-year-old children' by Carolyn Chaney
    (*Applied Psycholinguistics*, 1992)
'Phonological recoding and self-teaching: Sine qua non of reading
    acquisition' by David Share (*Cognition*, 1995)
'Is there a causal link from phonological awareness to success
    in learning to read?' by Anne Castles and Max Coltheart
    (*Cognition*, 2004)

The alphabetic code

The alphabetic code, or principle, refers to the understanding that letters are used to represent the speech sounds of our language. We use the letters of the alphabet often alone (the basic code), as well as in twos and in groups of three and four (advanced code), to represent the sounds in our language. Learning to read and write in English is far more difficult than in other languages. In the English language there is not a direct correspondence between the 26 letters of the alphabet and the approximately 44 phonemes. In other languages this is not the case and the codes are more transparent. Finnish, for example, is nearly completely regular, as are Italian, Swedish, Norwegian and German.

The English alphabetic code

Subject facts

It is the complexity of the English alphabetic code that has led to reluctance to teach phonics in the past, together with a lack of clear understanding by teachers of the advanced code. The English alphabetic code is underpinned by the following concepts.

● **Sounds/phonemes are represented by letters/graphemes:**
A phoneme can be represented by one or more letters, for example the phoneme /oa/ can be written as 'oa' (as in *boat*), 'o–e' (as in *phone*), or 'o' (as in *nose*). A one-letter grapheme is called a 'graph', a two-letter grapheme a 'digraph' and a three-letter grapheme a 'trigraph'. There are also four-letter graphemes known as 'quadgraphs' such as 'eigh' and 'aigh' (as in *eight* and *straight*).

● **The same phoneme can be represented (spelled) more than one way:** For example, the phoneme /ai/ can be written as 'ay' in play, or 'a–e' as in *make*, or 'ai' as in *trail*, or 'a' as in *baby*.

● **The same grapheme (spelling) may represent more than one phoneme:** This can be demonstrated by the letter 'c' which may make the sound /s/ in *city* or /c/ in *cat*.

The 44 phonemes of the English language

There are generally agreed to be approximately 44 phonemes in the English language, although there are about 174 ways of spelling these! There are 24 consonant phonemes; 18 of these have a close match between the letter and the sound it represents in a word.

/b/ as in 'bed'	/j/ as in 'jam'	/s/ as in 'sun'
/c/ as in 'cat'	/l/ as in 'leg'	/t/ as in 'tap'
/d/ as in 'dog'	/m/ as in 'mat'	/v/ as in 'van'
/f/ as in 'fan'	/n/ as in 'net'	/w/ as in 'win'
/g/ as in 'get'	/p/ as in 'pig'	/y/ as in 'yes'
/h/ as in 'hat'	/r/ as in 'rat'	/z/ as in 'zip'

There are also six further consonant phonemes, which are all digraphs (two letters making one sound).

/sh/ as in 'ship'	/ng/ as in 'ring'	/th/ as in 'then'
/ch/ as in 'church'	/th/ as in 'thin'	/zh/ as in 'television'

Of the 20 vowel phonemes, there are five short vowels.

/a/ as in 'cat'	/i/ as in 'bit'	/u/ as in 'hut'
/e/ as in 'peg'	/o/ as in 'dog'	

Five long vowels where the vowel 'says the letter name'. These long-vowel phonemes can also be represented as 'split digraphs' (two letters split by a consonant, as in the 'ay' sound in *make*).

/ai/ as in 'day'	/igh/ as in 'night'	/oo/ as in 'food'
/ee/ as in 'feet'	/oa/ as in 'toad'	

Further to this are the following nine long-vowel phonemes:

/ar/ as in 'car'	/oo/ as in 'book'	/air/ as in 'hair'
/ur/ as in 'burn'	/ow/ as in 'cow'	/ear/ as in 'fear'
/or/ as in 'corn'	/oi/ as in 'coin'	/ure/ as in 'sure'

There is also one unstressed vowel, /ə/ the 'schwa' phoneme, pronounced as 'uh' is in *collar*.

The basic code

Children learning phonics need to start with the basic code – the concept that a single letter makes one sound. They need to begin by learning one spelling for each of the 44 phonemes in the English language. Most phonics programmes begin with consonant-vowel-consonant (CVC) words (for example *cat*, *pin* and so on). However, it is important that they progress quickly to the more complex alphabetic code, which helps understanding of the alternative ways of representing the 44 phonemes. Problems have occurred in the past when phonics teaching focused on 'one letter makes one sound' and children rapidly realised that it did not always work, most notably with their own names, for example, 'Chloe', 'Philippa', and 'Sean'. If teaching does not move swiftly from the basic to the complex code, then children will not be able to 'crack the code' of learning to read and write in English.

The complex code

The principles of the complex code are that it involves the representation of a phoneme by one or sometimes more letters; the same phonemes can be spelled differently; and the same grapheme can represent different phonemes. The examples below examine these concepts in more depth:

1. One phoneme – one or more letters

The chart below demonstrates the frequency of phonemes represented by more than one letter.

The alphabetic code

Phonemes	Common spellings
/s/	sun, mouse, city, mess, science, mice
/a/	apple
/t/	tap, better
/p/	paper, hippo
/i/	ink, bucket
/n/	noise, knife, gnat
/e/	egg, bread
/d/	dog, puddle
/m/	man, hammer, comb
/g/	game, egg
/o/	octopus, want
/c/ /k/	cat, Chris, king, luck, queen
/u/	umbrella, love
/r/	rabbit, wrong, berry
/b/	baby, cabbage
/f/	fish, photo, coffee
/l/	leg, spell
/sh/	ship, mission, chef
/z/	zebra, please, is, fizzy, sneeze
/w/	water, wheel, queen
/ch/	chip, watch
/j/	jug, judge, giant, barge
/v/	van, drive
/h/	hat, hear, hot, hug, heel
/y/	yes, yoghurt, yawn, yell

Phonemes	Common spellings
/th/	thin, thumb, moth
/th/	then, that, with
/ng/	ring, sink
/zh/	treasure, vision
/ai/	play, take, snail, baby
/ee/	feel, heat, me, pony
/igh/	tie, fight, my, bike, tiger
/oa/	float, slow, stone, nose
/oo/	room, clue, grew, tune
/oo/	took, could, put
/ar/	car, fast (regional)
/ur/	fur, girl, term, heard, work
/or/	sauce, horn, door, warn, claw, ball
/ow/	cow, loud
/oi/	coin, boy
/air/	hair, bear, share
/ear/	ear, here, deer
/ure/	sure, tour
/ə/	teacher, collar, doctor, about

2. The same phoneme – different spelling

Look at the example below to see how many ways the phoneme /s/ can be represented in spelling.

Phoneme	Common spellings
/s/	's', 'se', 'c', 'ss', 'sc', 'ce'

3. The same grapheme – different phoneme

To make this more complex the same spelling or grapheme can represent different sounds or phonemes, as the example below shows:

Grapheme	Phoneme
ch	/ch/ in 'church' or /sh/ in 'chef'

Understanding the reversibility of the alphabetic code

The translation of the phonemes into graphemes is the basis of the English language writing system. The alphabetic code also works in reverse direction for reading where graphemes are translated into phonemes and the phonemes are then blended together (synthesised) to create the spoken words.

Letter names

Teaching letter names alongside the sounds has caused considerable debate. It is important not to confuse children, however one approach that clearly differentiates letters from sounds is to teach children that a letter has a name and that this letter also makes a sound. If the alphabet and letter names are taught very early, this knowledge can act as a basis for new knowledge, particularly when children learn that the same letter can make different sounds. Some phonics schemes delay teaching letter names and begin with the sounds, however, many children come to school knowing letter names from alphabet songs or friezes or from popular children's television programmes. If children already know these, it seems sensible to use them as an 'anchor' for new knowledge about sounds.

Why you need to know these facts

- Understanding the alphabetic code is the basis of understanding and teaching phonics. Knowing how to teach the alphabetic code by breaking it down into the basic and more complex aspects is fundamental.

● It is important to recognise the reversibility of the alphabetic code: for children to fully develop their phonic skills, they need to apply them both in reading and in writing. Every phonics lesson should provide opportunities for application in these different ways.

● Having a clear understanding of the common difficulties faced when teaching and learning phonics helps ensure that these are addressed. For some teachers these issues can impact on their own confidence and competence, however understanding how the alphabetic code works can help overcome this.

Vocabulary

Alphabetic code – the system or principle by which letters are used to represent the speech sounds of our language.
CVC word – consonant-vowel-consonant words, such as *pat*.
Digraph – two letters that combine to make a new sound.
Graph – one letter that makes one sound.
Quadgraph – four letters which combine to make a new sound.
Split digraph – two letters, making one sound, which are split by a consonant letter, for example 'a–e' as in *cake*.
Trigraph – three letters that combine to make a new sound.

Common misconceptions

One common misconception, particularly for adults, is that the number of phonemes and graphemes varies in a word. There is always the same number of phonemes as graphemes. So, for example, a word such as *light* represents the following phonemes: /l/ /igh/ /t/ (three phonemes and three graphemes). A grapheme may consist of one, two, three or occasionally four letters.

Questions

What are the three key factors of the English complex alphabetic code?

The three factors that account for the complex English alphabetic code are:

- phonemes can be represented by one, two, three or occasionally four letters
- phonemes can be spelled in different ways
- a grapheme may represent different phonemes.

Handy tip

The International Phonetic Alphabet (IPA), which is shown in Chapter 4 and is also found at the front of dictionaries such as the *Oxford English Dictionary*, can be a very useful tool when there is any confusion identifying individual phonemes.

Teaching ideas

Most phonics programmes begin with teaching the basic code, typically 's', 'a', 't', 'p', 'i', 'n'. These grapheme/phoneme correspondences can very quickly be used to make CVC words, thus providing essential practice in applying the knowledge by blending the phonemes together to make words and using the reversible process of segmenting words (for example *pat* = /p/ /a/ /t/) to spell them. Some effective strategies for teaching the basic code are given below.

● Hear it, say it, read it, write it! It is important for children to be able to accurately hear a phoneme, say it or pronounce it correctly and to be able to apply this knowledge in reading the corresponding grapheme and writing it using correct letter formation. The order of teaching for the basic code should therefore be as follows:

1. Say a number of words that contain a chosen phoneme (to begin with, the focus will be on the phoneme in the initial position in the word, for example, for /s/, *sun*, *sip* and *sat*).
2. Help children to say the phoneme, emphasising the correct pronunciation and, where appropriate, stretching the sound, for example: /sssssssssssss/. (See the following section on the pronunciation of phonemes.)
3. Read the grapheme that represents the phoneme, ensuring that children can clearly see it (pointing to it clearly or using an interactive whiteboard to display it).
4. Write the corresponding grapheme, teaching the correct letter formation, using instructions such as 'straight down' for a letter such as 'l', or 'straight down and back up again' for other letters such as 'n' and anticlockwise movements for letters such as 'c'.

● Phoneme frames are one way of supporting children to segment words into phonemes and can be an effective teaching tool. Children segment the graphemes of words into the corresponding phonemes by writing the graphemes in separate boxes. A laminated sheet, or an individual whiteboard with separate boxes drawn on so that children can write with a dry-wipe pen, is ideal. A word is said aloud by the teacher, then the child says it slowly, segmenting it into phonemes, and then writes the corresponding graphemes. For example, for *sit* a child writes:

s	i	t

● Phoneme fingers are another way of supporting children in practising segmenting words into phonemes. Here a word is said aloud, the children are asked to repeat it and then to count individually the number of phonemes on their fingers as they say it. They then show the teacher how many 'phoneme fingers', or phonemes, are in a word. Children may also pretend to write the letters on each finger to represent each phoneme.

● Phoneme buttons are where you present a written version of the word which can be displayed on an individual whiteboard, an easel or an interactive whiteboard. Children place 'buttons' or dots underneath each phoneme, for example:

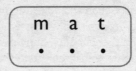

● Segmenting a word into its constituent phonemes is a complex skill which can be helped by introducing the idea of talking like a robot. Children may be familiar with 'daleks' through the *Dr Who* TV programme. Hearing talk in a staccato way, like a dalek, can be a useful way to begin to understand the idea of talking like a robot. To introduce this to children, the following idea may be helpful.

Robbie Robot

Show a picture of a robot and tell the children that he can only talk in phonemes. The robot could be given a name, such as 'Robbie Robot'. The following is an example of how this might be done using 'robot talk':

> This is Robbie and because he is a robot, he talks in a strange way – a bit like a dalek. Let's hear him talk:
> /s/ /a/ /d/ (Hold up the picture of the robot and pretend it is talking.)
> What do you think he said? Can you repeat it?
> Yes /s/ /a/ /d/. What does he mean? Is he sad? Well done!
> Yes he says 'sad'.
> Now he does not understand you unless you talk like a robot.
> You need to say the sounds, remember we call them phonemes, separately. Shall we have a go?
> Let's try with 'pin'. (Prompt children to speak in robot talk.)
> Good, it's /p/ /i/ /n/. Can you say that to Robbie? Let's see if he says it back to you.
> /p/ /i/ /n/ (Hold up the picture of the robot and pretend it is talking.)
> Well done! Remember, when we talk to Robbie we must talk in phonemes.

Once the idea of 'robot talk' has been introduced it can be

incorporated into all phonics sessions, so that children have the opportunity to practise segmenting words into their constituent phonemes alongside blending them for reading. The main aim of learning to segment words is to support children's ability to spell words, so it should be introduced early in a systematic phonics programme, followed by frequent opportunities to practise.

Pronunciation of phonemes

Subject facts

It is very important that teachers model the correct pronunciation or enunciation of phonemes when teaching. The most common error is to add an 'uh' sound to phonemes (as in 'r', often pronounced 'ruh'). While it is difficult to pronounce some phonemes purely, every effort should be made to eliminate extra sounds. One way to help this is to appreciate that some phonemes are 'sustained' or 'stretched' phonemes and can be pronounced purely as listed below. A pronunciation chart is provided in the Appendix, showing in detail how to say the sounds purely.

- **Sustained sounds:** all vowel phonemes plus /f/, /l/, /m/, /n/, /r/, /s/, /v/, /z/, /th/ (unvoiced), /th/ (voiced), /ng/, /sh/.

- **Unsustained sounds:** The other phonemes should be pronounced as purely as possible. For voiced sounds (where the voice vibrates) children can put fingers on their throats to feel the vibration and for unvoiced sounds (/c/, /t/, /p/, /ch/) they can whisper them, which helps to keep the sound pure.

- **Schwa:** The 'schwa' phoneme /ə/ is the most common sound in our language and has the greatest variation. It causes two principal problems, first the sheer variety of ways of spelling it: 'er' in *teacher*, 'e' in *wooden*, 'u' in *circus*, 'ar' in *collar*, 'or' in *doctor*. The second problem is that in enunciating phonemes it is important to pronounce them without the 'schwa', an unstressed vowel or extra sound added to some phonemes. Ofsted has reiterated the importance of this:

Correct articulation is vital in helping children to learn to blend sounds together. This means making sure that the sound produced (each individual phoneme) is as precise and accurate as possible and that no additional sounds are added. For instance, the sound /m/ that starts 'mother' or is embedded in 'impress' needs to sound /mmmm/ and not /muh/. The clearer the sound, the easier it is for a child to blend together (synthesise) the individual sounds to read a word because there are no unnecessary sounds getting in the way.

Getting Them Reading Early (Ofsted, 2011)

Accent and dialect

One aspect that can cause difficulty when teaching phonics relates to regional pronunciation. Teachers find this particularly problematic when their accent is different from that of the children they are teaching. Language experts such as David Crystal maintain that what we describe as Standard English may be 'spoken in a vast range of regional accents'. However, Ruth Miskin, who has produced a well-known phonics programme (*Read, Write, Inc.*), maintains that 'all but four or five of the 44 sounds are pronounced consistently across all accents'. Many teachers find it necessary to adjust their accent to be similar to the children's when teaching phonics, so if teaching in the North of England, a teacher would say *grass* with a short vowel sound, /a/, rather than *grass* with a long vowel sound, /ar/, even if he or she came from the South of England, in order to ensure children are not confused by this.

Why you need to know these facts

● Having a clear understanding of the need to enunciate phonemes purely is important to avoid any incorrect pronunciation, such as the additional sound 'uh' being added to phonemes, which may then lead to incorrect blending of sounds. It also helps in ensuring that correct pronunciation is modelled and taught to young children.

Vocabulary

Schwa /ə/ – the most common vowel sound in English, it has multiple spellings and is often described as 'weak' as it occurs in unstressed syllables in words. Examples include the final sound in *teacher* and *collar*.

Unvoiced – a sound that is made without using the vocal chords.

Voiced – a sound that is made using the vocal chords.

Amazing facts

The schwa is the most common sound in English. It is difficult to distinguish as it is unstressed within syllables in words and it can be spelled in a number of ways using different vowels, for example:

- 'a' in *adept*
- 'e' in *wooden*
- 'i' in *decimal*
- 'o' in *harmony*
- 'y' in *syringe*.

Often the vowel letter is accompanied by 'r' as in *dollar, teacher,* and *doctor*.

Handy tip

In order to decide whether a sound is voiced or unvoiced, put your fingers on your throat and then experiment with different sounds. Try *thing* and *these* to see the difference. When you feel a vibration with your fingers, the sound is made using your vocal chords and is 'voiced'.

Teaching ideas

● Ensure correct modelling of sounds. Make use of a range of video guides, for example *Mr Thorne Does Phonics* (www.mrthorne.com). Provide plenty of practice with opportunities to check children are enunciating correctly.

● Use the pronunciation guide provided in the Appendix to teach physical aspects, such as the placing of the tongue in the mouth; the shaping of the lips; and the voiced or unvoiced nature of some sounds, demonstrated by placing hands on the throat to feel the vibration.

Resources

Quick Fix for Phonics by Wendy Jolliffe (Scholastic)
How Language Works by David Crystal (Penguin)
Getting Them Reading Early (Ofsted, 2011)
Read Write Inc. Phonics Handbook by Ruth Miskin
    (Oxford University Press)
Mr Thorne Does Phonics – www.mrthorne.com

Long-vowel phonemes

Long-vowel phonemes are the most complex aspect of teaching phonics and a lack of understanding means that they are sometimes not well taught. Considering the fact that there are 14 of them, often digraphs or trigraphs, and also that these can be spelled in multiple ways, this is not surprising. Without a clear understanding of this important area, however, the ability to utilise phonics for reading and writing is severely limited. Long-vowel phonemes provide a crucial part of the alphabetic code. In spite of their complexity it is possible to teach young children these phonemes and their corresponding graphemes, using multi-sensory methods, and for children to develop a good understanding of the phonetic structure of the English language.

Understanding long-vowel phonemes

Subject facts

Long-vowel phonemes, as the term implies, represent the long vowel sounds in English, for example /ai/ in *hay* and *play*. While many children, and adults, know there are five vowels in English, most do not realise that there are a total of 20 vowel sounds and, of these, only five are the short vowel sounds that correspond to the vowel letters (/a/, /e/, /i/, /o/ and /u/). The chart on the next page sets out all these phonemes with their common spellings.

Long-vowel phonemes

Phonemes	Graphemes	Common spellings
/ai/	ay, a–e, ai, a	play, take, snail, baby
/ee/	ee, ea, e	feel, heat, me
/igh/	ie, igh, y, i–e, i	tie, fight, my, bike, tiger
/oa/	oa, ow, o–e, o	float, slow, stone, nose
/oo/	oo, ou, u	took, could, put
/oo/	oo, ue, ew, u–e	room, clue, grew, tune
/ow/	ow, ou	cow, loud
/oi/	oi, oy	coin, boy
/ur/	u, ir, er, ear, or	fur, girl, term, heard, work
/or/	au, or, oor, ar, aw, a	sauce, horn, door, warn, claw, ball
/ar/	ar, a	car, fast (regional)
/air/	air, ear, are	hair, bear, share
/ear/	ear, ere, eer	ear, here, deer
/ure/	ure, our	sure, tour
/ə/	er, ar, or, a	teacher, collar, doctor, about, garden, fungus

The schwa phoneme /ə/

The schwa phoneme, most commonly written as 'er', as in *sister*, is one of the most complex phonemes in the English language and further complicates the teaching of long-vowel phonemes. This is because it is contained in words of more than one syllable: it is the unstressed vowel in such words and it can be written in many ways. As the phoneme is unstressed, it is often difficult to hear and to differentiate correctly. The common alternatives are 'ar' (as in *collar*), 'e' (as in *garden*), 'u' (as in the second 'u' of *fungus*) and 'or' (as in *doctor*).

Split digraphs

Vowel digraphs in English are sometimes 'split'; that is, the graphemes representing the phoneme are divided by a consonant, for example in the word *cake*, the vowel digraph for /ai/ is written as 'a–e', with the 'a' and the 'e' split by the letter 'k', representing the /k/ sound. However, when you segment the word *cake* it is 'c' 'a–e' 'k'.

Common spelling patterns

Considering the complexity of the phonetic structure of the English language, it is surprising to discover that it does contain stable spellings and stable pronunciations. 'Rimes' are a good example of this. A rime is the final part of a word and consists of the vowel sound plus the final consonant: in a word such as *hate* the rime is '-ate'. The initial part of the word (in this case 'h-') is called the 'onset' of the word. The onset of a word may include more than one consonant, as in the 'pl-' in *plate*. A child would find it easier to decode the word 'plate' having encountered the word *hate*, as the rime '-ate' has a stable spelling and pronunciation.

The use of onset and rime, largely derived from the work of Usha Goswami, became very popular as the focus for teaching reading. This approach is what is termed 'analytic phonics', where words are decoded based on inference from words with similar spelling patterns. As a method of teaching reading this has drawbacks in that it does not systematically teach all 44-plus phonemes and their alternative spellings and pronunciations. However, where this has real value is in demonstrating the stable patterns in our language.

In total, there are approximately 174 common spelling patterns. These patterns are particularly useful in teaching spelling. Research by Linnea C Ehri has shown that the brain is a pattern detector and when a pattern is detected in a word, it evokes associations, for example the word *complaint* may be associated with *mail*, *paint* and *constraint*. The table on the next page (from 'Teaching Vowels Through Phonograms' by Richard E Wylie and Donald D Durrell) provides a list of 37 rimes that provide nearly 500 words in English:

Long-vowel phonemes

-ack	-ain	-ake	-ale
-all	-ame	-an	-ank
-ap	-ash	-at	-ate
-aw	-ay	-eat	-ell
-est	-ice	-ick	-ide
-ite	-ill	-in	-ine
-ing	-ink	-ip	-ir
-ock	-oke	-op	-or
-ore	-uck	-ug	-ump
-unk			

The International Phonetic Alphabet (IPA)

The development of an international phonetic alphabet by the International Phonetic Association aimed to provide a notational standard for the phonetic representation of all languages.
The Association began its work in 1886 and the latest version of the IPA was produced in 2005. The chart is particularly useful in understanding and teaching phonics and it is also used by the DfE in its guidance related to the phonics screening test for six-year-olds.

Consonants

Phoneme	Example	Phoneme	Example
/b/	bad	/ŋ/	sing
/d/	dog	/θ/	both
/ð/	this	/p/	pet
/dʒ/	gem, jug	/r/	red
/f/	if, puff, photo	/s/	sit, miss, cell
/g/	gum	/ʃ/	she, chef
/h/	how	/t/	tea
/j/	yes	/tʃ/	check

Phoneme	Example	Phoneme	Example
/k/	cat, check, key, school	/v/	vet
		/w/	wet, when
/l/	leg, hill	/z/	zip, hens, buzz
/m/	man	/ʒ/	pleasure*
/n/	man		

* Not included in the phonics screening check

Vowels

Phoneme	Graphemes	Phoneme	Graphemes
/ɑː/	father, arm	/iː/	she, bead, see,
/ɒ/	hot		scheme, chief
/æ/	cat		launch, raw,
/aɪ/	mind, fine, pie, high	/ɔː/	born
			coin, boy
/aʊ/	out, cow	/ɔɪ/	book^, cup^,
/ɛ/	hen, head^	/ʊ/	could
/eɪ/	say, came, bait		tour*
	air	/ʊə/	stew, room, you,
/ɛə/	cold, boat, cone,	/uː/	blue,
/əʊ/	mould, blow		brute
	hit	/ʌ/	cup^
/ɪ/	beer*	/ɜː/	fern, turn, girl
/ɪə/		/ə/	farmer

^ This grapheme/phoneme correspondence (GPC) only applies to certain regional pronunciations
* Not included in the phonics screening check

Why you need to know these facts

● In order to fully understand phonics, it is important to have a clear grasp of the long-vowel phonemes and their multiple spelling choices. This is the key to effective application of phonics to reading and writing. This helps explain the seemingly random nature of our spelling system.

● While analytic phonics is no longer a recommended approach for the teaching of reading, it is helpful to look at stable spelling patterns when teaching spelling.

Vocabulary

Consonant digraph – two letters representing a consonant phoneme, for example 'ph' in *graph*, 'wh' in *why* and 'gh' in *laugh*.
Onset – in analytic phonics, this is the first part of a word: the consonant or adjacent consonants at the beginning and before the vowel, for example 'fl-' in *flat*.
Rime – in analytic phonics, this is the final part of the word: the vowel sound and any consonant sounds that follow it, for example '-at' in *flat*.

Amazing facts

The English spelling system, or orthography, has evolved due to the influences of a number of cultures and a series of invasions by other countries. From its Celtic origins to the influence of Latin (known as 'vulgar Latin' – its spoken form) during the Roman occupation, German from the Anglo Saxon invasion and the Scandinavian languages from the Vikings, we can begin to understand how English has developed. After the Norman Conquest in 1066, French was imposed as the language of the rulers of the country, although most documents were written in Latin. When printing developed in the 15th century, many early printers were German or Dutch and brought their own spellings to texts. In the 17th century, a standard spelling system was still not in place, and scholars began to modify the way in which they spelled some words to reflect their classical origins, so that words such as *receipt* acquired a 'p'; *rime* became *rhyme*; and *rein* became *reign* with a 'g' from the Latin 'regno'. This history helps explain the idiosyncratic nature of English spelling.

In the past, there were attempts to simplify the English alphabetic code for the purposes of teaching children to read. One of the most notable ones, the Initial Teaching Alphabet

(ITA), was devised by Sir James Pitman (1961) and comprised a restructuring of the alphabet with additions made to cover the 44 phonemes. Children learned the sound–symbol correspondences and were provided with texts in which words were written in the Initial Teaching Alphabet as shown below:

b	c	d	f	g	h
bed	cat	dog	fish	goat	hat
j	k	l	m	n	p
jug	key	lion	man	nest	pet
r	s	t	v	w	y
rock	sun	table	voice	win	yet
z	a	e	i	o	u
zip	apple	engine	insect	hot	umbrella
æ	é	í	œ	ú	ù
angel	eel	ice	oat	uniform	wheel
ç	š	þ	ð	â	ò
chair	shoe	thumb	that	auto	oil
ó	ñ	ž	ý	û	à
owl	ring	dogs	garage	bird	father
õ	ô				
book	moon				

This system, while innovative, presented a number of drawbacks and was discontinued as a method of teaching. The drawbacks included the lack of reading materials written using this system and the problems children encountered when attempting to move on to traditional English spelling.

Long-vowel phonemes

Common misconceptions

One misconception is that spelling is developed through reading, and advice to poor spellers has often been to read more. However, as David Crystal (see Resources) has shown, spelling involves a different ability from whole-word reading, which relies on visual pattern recognition. Instead, spelling requires both phonological awareness that supports knowledge of spelling patterns and a good visual awareness to support exceptions. Systematic teaching of phonics is a vital aspect of learning to be a good speller.

Questions

What are the key reasons why long-vowel phonemes are so complex?
This is because there are 14 long-vowel phonemes in addition to the schwa sound, which can be spelled in a number of ways, commonly using digraphs and split digraphs.

How have the many spelling choices for the long-vowel phonemes evolved?
The different spelling choices for the long-vowel phonemes have evolved due to many different cultural influences and invasions of England through the ages.

Why is the International Phonetic Alphabet useful in understanding the phonetic structure of our language and its representations?
The International Phonetic Alphabet is useful in providing a stable representation of the phonemes or sounds, which helps in checking the numbers of phonemes in words. It has been an important development during the last century to have a universal system of symbols to represent the sounds of the language.

Teaching ideas

● Teaching all 20 vowel phonemes is important. The easiest way to approach this is to begin by teaching the five short-vowel phonemes (/a/, /e/, /i/, /o/, /u/) and then work systematically through the remainder, as shown on the chart at the beginning of this chapter.

● You may decide to teach the most common representation of each of the long-vowel phonemes first (which is shown as the first one among the common spellings) and then later teach the other ways of spelling the phoneme.

● A particularly effective way to support children in learning long-vowel phonemes is to create a chart of phonemes as each one is taught. This should begin by focusing on the most common graphemes for each phoneme first and adding those that are most appropriate for the age of the children. The key is to gradually build a chart as each grapheme, or representation of the same phoneme, is taught. In this way a large chart can be created for reference, with each component understood as it is built up. This may include pictures to represent each phoneme to make the chart both more useful and more attractive. A completed chart is given below. For more guidance on teaching this, with detailed lesson plans, see *Quick Fix for Phonics* (Scholastic).

Phonemes	Graphemes					
/ai/	ay (day)	ai (tail)	a (baby)	a–e (make)		
/ee/	ee (see)	ea (beach)	e (me)	y (pony)		
/igh/	ie (tie)	igh (light)	y (my)	i (tiger)	i–e (time)	
/oa/	oa (boat)	ow (snow)	o (cold)	o–e (bone)		
/oo/	oo (book)	ou (would)	u (put)			

Long-vowel phonemes

/oo/	oo (moon)	ue (clue)	ew (grew)	u–e (tune)		
/ow/	ow (cow)	ou (shout)				
/oi/	oi (coin)	oy (boy)				
/ur/	ur (burn)	ir (girl)	er (term)	ear (heard)	or (work)	
/or/	au (haul)	or (horn)	oor (door)	ar (warn)	aw (claw)	a (call)
/ar/	ar (car)	a (fast)				
/air/	air (hair)	ear (bear)	are (share)			
/ear/	ear (fear)	ere (here)	eer (deer)			
/ure/	ure (sure)	our (tour)				
/ə/	er (sister)	e (wooden)	u (circus)	a (about)	ar (collar)	or (doctor)

● Research studies show that the use of multi-sensory teaching methods can aid children's learning and retention of grapheme/phoneme correspondences (GPCs). These include the use of actions, mnemonics, songs, raps and rhymes, and visual prompts for each GPC. It is important to be consistent in teaching the same actions for a phoneme. Guidance from a particular scheme, for example *Quick Fix for Phonics* (Scholastic) or *Jolly Phonics* (Jolly Learning), may be helpful.

● In order to help young children to recall these phonemes, learning a saying or mnemonic can be helpful. This can also be accompanied by an action. As the phonemes are learned, these sayings can be linked together to form a 'rap'. Said in a lively way at the start of each phonics lesson, it can be a fun introduction and acts as revision of the phonemes taught. Constant practice at saying this rap will support children in remembering the phonemes and the most common graphemes. When teaching the rap, it is important to observe the following steps:

1. Say the phoneme twice, for example /ai/, /ai/.
2. Say the mnemonic, for example 'Play with hay'.
3. Say the letter names, for example 'A, Y'.

When accompanied by an action, this would look as follows:

	Phoneme — say twice (grapheme in brackets)	Phrase	Letter names	Action
/ai/	/ai/, /ai/ ('ay', 'ay')	Play with hay	A, Y	Pretend to lift a pile of hay
	/ai/, /ai/ ('ai', 'ai')	Ai, ai what did you say?	A, I	Hand cupped around ear
	/ai/, /ai/ ('a', 'a')	Acorn in an acre	A	Pretend to hold a tiny acorn
/ee/	/ee/, /ee/ ('ee', 'ee')	Feel the tree	E, E	Pretend to hug a tree
	/ee/, /ee/ ('ea', 'ea')	Heat the meat	E, A	Pretend to stir with a spoon
	/ee/, /ee/ ('e', 'e')	He and me	E	Point to someone
	/ee/, /ee/ ('y', 'y')	Bony pony	Y	Pretend to ride a pony
/igh/	/igh/, /igh/ ('ie', 'ie')	Tie the tie	I, E	Pretend to tie a tie
	/igh/, /igh/ ('igh', 'igh')	Light helps sight	I, G, H	Make a circle with thumb and forefinger and hold around eyes
	/igh/, /igh/ ('y', 'y')	My what a fly	Y	Buzz like a fly
	/igh/, /igh/ ('i', 'i')	Kind tiger	I	Pretend to wave to a tiger

For full details of the rap see *Quick Fix for Phonics* by Wendy Jolliffe.

● The use of visual aids can also support learning long-vowel phonemes. For a version including images see *Quick Fix for Phonics* by Wendy Jolliffe (Scholastic). The diagram below provides an example.

ay	ai
'ay' 'ay' Play with hay AY	'ai' 'ai' What did you say? AI

a	ee
'a' 'a' Acorn in an acre A	'ee' 'ee' Feel the tree EE

● Learning phonics, and particularly the long-vowel phonemes, requires systematic teaching combined with opportunities for over-learning. This can be done each day and built on as you learn a new phoneme. If you learn in the form of a rap, as suggested previously, this can be a fun way of starting each phonics session.

Working with parents

Subject facts

To support children in becoming proficient with synthetic phonics, it is extremely important to provide clear information for parents in order to help them understand the process their children will be undertaking. A range of resources is available to help this, including booklets for parents published by phonics programmes. The booklet *Letters and Sounds: Phonics information for parents and carers with children in Reception classes* provides a range of activities that parents can undertake with children at each phase and can be downloaded from the internet (see Resources).

Why you need to know these facts

● Phonics is complex and it needs reinforcement regularly so it is important for parents to be able to do this at home. Parents need guidance on how to do this in order not to confuse children. One example is in the correct enunciation of phonemes. The common mistake is to add the 'uh' sound to phonemes so that 'm' becomes 'muh'. This is adding an additional sound, which will be problematic when children start to blend the phonemes.

Teaching ideas

● Parents need guidance on correct pronunciation. Provide them with a pronunciation guide (see Appendix) and ensure that they realise the phonemes should be pronounced as purely as possible, avoiding 'uh' as in 'muh' or 'ruh'.

● Parents also need to clearly understand that they should not confuse children by using letter names and sounds at the same time. Clear explanation of the role of both is needed and it is also important to tell them that, for reading, children need to learn the sounds and then blend the sounds together.

● Show parents how to play phonics games that will help their children to use their phonic knowledge as the prime method of decoding text. For example, play 'I spy something beginning with…' using the phoneme instead of the letter name, or talk in phonemes (as in 'robot talk' – see Chapter 3) and then blending the phonemes into words.

● Reinforce to parents that it is important for children to continue enjoying a wealth of children's books, and that they should provide frequent opportunities for their children to listen to stories and jointly explore books and illustrations.

Resources

Quick Fix for Phonics by Wendy Jolliffe (Scholastic)
Mother Tongue: The Story of the English Language by Bill Bryson (Penguin)
How Language Works by David Crystal (Penguin)
'Development of Sight Word Reading: Phases and findings' by Linnea C Ehri in *The Science of Reading* by Margaret Snowling and Charles Hulme (Blackwell)
'Teaching Vowels Through Phonograms' by Richard E Wylie and Donald D Durrell (*Elementary English*, 1970)
A range of resources for working in partnership with parents, including *Letters and Sounds: Phonics information for parents and carers with children in Reception classes*, are available from www.teachfind.com - search for 'Letters and sounds parents'.

Application of phonics

The application of phonics in reading and writing is one of the keys to successfully learning phonics. This should begin as soon as the first few phonemes are taught, to encourage young children to see the connection between learning the grapheme/ phoneme correspondences (GPCs) and reading and writing text. To aid this, most phonics programmes begin by teaching a few consonant sounds and some short vowels: /s/, /a/, /t/, /p/, /i/, /n/. These GPCs can then be applied in reading and writing a number of consonant-vowel-consonant (CVC) words, such as *pat, sip, tin* and so on. The draft National Curriculum for English, cites the advantages:

> *Practice at reading such words by sounding and blending can provide opportunities not only for pupils to develop confidence in their decoding skills but also for teachers to explain the meaning and thus develop pupils' vocabulary.*

Segmenting and blending

Subject facts

How to apply known GPCs for reading, along with the skill of blending them together to read a word, needs to be taught early in any phonics programme and to be followed up with frequent practice. Every phonics lesson needs to provide opportunities to practise reading known and new phonemes in a variety of ways. A range of teaching ideas is provided below. The application of phonics in reading, generally involves recognising the grapheme, knowing its corresponding phoneme, continuing this process for all the graphemes in a word and then blending the phonemes together to read the word.

For writing, the application is reversed: first the word needs to be segmented into its individual phonemes and then the graphemes relating to the corresponding phonemes need to be recalled and finally written. However, it should be noted that while reading involves blending and spelling involves segmenting, both are intimately connected. For experienced readers the process happens at a phenomenal speed – the same sound-by-sound analysis happens, but the speed makes for automaticity. Skilled readers only become aware of this interplay when they encounter a word they cannot read or spell.

This interrelationship becomes clear when we realise that spelling has a fundamental success rate in relation to reading. The very first literacy programmes started with teaching spelling, and pioneers, such as Maria Montessori in 1912, advised teachers to teach spelling first and then for children to use this to read what they have written.

Being able to blend phonemes has been shown by research to make a significant difference to a child's success in learning to read. Research in 2005 by the Primary National Strategy found that at that time there was little teaching of blending in schools. Much emphasis has been placed on this since, for example with the DCSF *Letters and Sounds* phonics materials. It is important to give children plenty of practice of blending. This can be done by the adult saying the phonemes and, following some modelling of how to blend, asking the children to blend them into words. For example, the adult says: /f/ /i/ /sh/ and then the children say *fish*. 'Robot talk' can also help with this (see Chapter 3).

Segmentation is the corresponding skill to blending and requires children to segment or divide words into the constituent phonemes: for example, the word *stand* consists of five phonemes: /s/ /t/ /a/ /n/ /d/. In order to be able to write words children need to apply this process. As phonic knowledge develops and children know at least one grapheme correspondence for each of the 44-plus phonemes, work then needs to be done on selecting appropriate spelling choices for phonemes, with children gradually internalising the orthographic patterns of our language to make the correct choices. In other words, learning phonics later merges into learning spelling and many phonics programmes provide guidance on this in later stages, such as in phases 5 and 6 of *Letters and Sounds*.

Segmenting and blending are related to the processes of decoding and encoding text. Decoding requires reading of the symbols or letters and transferring them into sounds to recover the words. Therefore, when decoding we sound out the letters and blend them together to make a word. Encoding involves spelling and is the process of turning sounds into symbols or letters. As in segmenting and blending, these processes of decoding and encoding are reversible and it is crucial, when teaching young children, that we make this explicit by providing opportunities to both read and write graphemes for the corresponding phonemes during every phonics teaching session. This reversibility can support spelling, as it is important to realise that we can always read words we can spell, but we cannot always spell words we can read. However, while these two processes are reversible, they require different skills.

Decoding, or reading, requires recognition memory as the letters act as a prompt for the phonemes. For encoding, there is no visual prompt and the child must use recall memory, which is more difficult. To spell a word, a child needs to carry out the following tasks:

1. Identify the phonemes in the word (for example, *meat* /m/ /ee/ /t/ = three phonemes).
2. Recall the phonemes in the correct sequence (/m/ /ee/ /t/).
3. Remember how each phoneme is spelled (/m/ 'm', /ee/ 'ea', /t/ 't').
4. Write the correct grapheme to represent each phoneme (meat).

Why you need to know these facts

● Having a clear understanding of the interrelationship between segmenting and blending helps to ensure that both aspects are included in all phonics teaching. It also helps in realising that teaching phonics has advantages for both reading and writing. It is often mistakenly felt that phonics principally refers to reading. In fact segmenting and blending are reversible skills: reading requires the skill of recognising the letters and their corresponding sounds and then blending these phonemes together into words; in contrast, spelling requires the opposite – the words are segmented into their corresponding sounds or phonemes and then the graphemes, or letters, are written. It is also important to understand that these skills need teaching and that, for young children, blending phonemes and segmenting words into phonemes requires careful modelling and plenty of practice.

Teaching ideas

Constant practice will be needed in order to help children move from the rather staccato sounds they make in response to reading letters, to blending them together into seamless words. The key to this is to explicitly model blending phonemes into words, ensuring children practise after hearing each word. They should be carefully observed doing this to ensure they are developing the skill of blending, and additional support should be provided where required.

● Require the children to say a password in order to do an action, such as go out to play, leave the room and so on. Tell them the constituent phonemes in a word first and when they want to do the action, they have to correctly whisper the word (the password) to you.

● Have a puppet that can only speak in phonemes. The puppet (of course, in reality, the adult!) tells the children a word in phonemes, for example /p/ /l/ /ai/, and the children have to orally blend the phonemes to say the word. Shared reading, as well as being a way of sharing the joy of reading a wide range of texts, is an invaluable tool in demonstrating how to decode texts using phonics. Many children's books include repeated refrains and particular words that children can decode phonetically. One good example of this is *Brown Bear, Brown Bear, What Do You See?* by Bill Martin and Eric Carle (Picture Puffin), in which the refrain, *Brown Bear, Brown Bear, what do you see?* is repeated, but with the substitution of names of successive birds and animals, and is followed by the refrain: *I see a… looking at me.*

● Guided reading is another important way of supporting children's ability to blend phonemes through using phonetically decodable books (see the section below on decodable texts for more information). This should not, however, prevent children from accessing the diverse world of children's literature through having frequent opportunities for being read to by an adult.

Another way of supporting children's early attempts at independent reading is through helping them to make their own books. Blank A5 books can be simply made by folding a sheet of A4 coloured paper and inserting inside two folded A4 pages and then stapling down the left-hand side. These books can then be used to record words and, later, sentences that children have read.

● Display a number of words that children will be able to read phonetically from the phonemes they have been taught, and ask them to order the words into sentences. An adult then writes the sentence in the child's book (or later the child can do this). The sentences can be used as practice for reading.

Decodable texts

Subject facts

The *Criteria for Assuring High-quality Phonic Work* (DfE, 2011) states that phonics teaching should ensure that as children move through the early stages of acquiring phonics, they practise by reading texts which are entirely decodable for them, so that they experience success and learn to rely on phonemic strategies. Decodable texts contain words that are at an appropriate phonemic level for children to decode.

Ideally, therefore, first-stage books would contain the consonant and short-vowel phonemes used in a number of simple CVC words. However, such texts are very limited and it is necessary to introduce a small number of common exception words such as *the*, *was* and *one* in order to create sentences that have some meaning and interest (see Chapter 6). It is important to limit the number of these words so that children are not using whole-word recognition as a frequent strategy for reading, but rather that their prime strategy is to decode using phonics.

Decodable texts provide vital practice for children in reading known phonemes and blending them into words. The draft National Curriculum guidance recommends that teachers should:

> *Ensure that pupils practise their reading with books that are consistent with their developing phonic knowledge and that do not require them to use other strategies to work out words.*

There has been considerable debate about the use of these texts. Academics have argued that very limited amounts of meaning and interest can be gained from such limited texts. One of the key aims of early reading is to foster a love of reading and some claim the use of decodable texts does exactly the opposite. However, the intention is not that children should be exposed solely to decodable texts: this is a small part of the varied diet they should be offered in a language-rich curriculum. The draft National Curriculum states that children should:

> *Develop pleasure in reading and motivation to read by...*
> *Listening to and discussing a wide range of poems and stories at a level beyond that which they can read independently.*

The Rose Report, *The Independent Review of the Teaching of Early Reading,* also set out the advantages of children using decodable books, saying:

> *this enables them to benefit from 'quick wins' in practising phonic skills and gaining confidence from reading a whole, albeit short, book.*

Why you need to know these facts

● It is important to understand how the use of decodable texts can improve children's phonic knowledge and skills. However, a wide range of children's texts should also be read to children for enjoyment and to improve their vocabulary and understanding of how texts work.

> ## Vocabulary

Common exception words – words that occur frequently in a language but that are irregular (not easily decodable using phonics), for example *said*, *their* and *one*.

> ## Teaching ideas

● The use of mini-books that contain simple decodable text at a level that is appropriate for young children is a valuable tool for practising blending phonemes. Books can also be created, as stated previously, by folding several A4 pages in half and stapling along the left-hand edge. On each page, simple sentences can be written using phonemes the children have been taught. For example, using the phonemes /s/, /a/, /t/, /p/, /i/, and /n/, these words can be created: *tap*, *sat*, *pin*, *at*, *pat*, *nap*, *nip*, *ant*, *pant*, *in* and *an*. Then, the following phrases and simple sentences could be written into mini-books:

An ant sat.
Pat an ant.
Sat on a pin.
Tap, tap, tap.
In a pin
In a tap
Nip, nip, nip…an ant.

Application for spelling

> ## Subject facts

Just as it is important to apply phonemes for reading, it is also important to apply them in writing or spelling. As stated previously, this requires segmenting words into phonemes and then writing the corresponding graphemes. Every lesson should include opportunities to write the GPCs being taught and those learned recently.

The draft National Curriculum notes and guidance for Year 1 emphasises that teachers should:

> *Ensure that spelling is taught alongside reading, so that pupils understand that they can read back words they have spelt.*

It also says that:

> *Writing simple dictated sentences that include words taught so far gives pupils opportunities to apply and practise their spelling knowledge.*

One of the key advantages of teaching systematic synthetic phonics is that it provides a clear foundation for developing spelling skills. Successful spellers make use of the knowledge and skills acquired through practising blending and segmenting words. In fact, early spelling largely involves phonics, which has a number of advantages:

- It is flexible as the same letters can be used to make different words.
- Children can attempt to spell words independently using their phonic knowledge.
- Each word does not need to be memorised.
- Although spelling attempts may not be correct, they are usually decodable, for example 'nyoo' for *new*.

Why you need to know these facts

- Using phonics is a key factor in becoming an effective speller as it provides a strategy for children to begin the complex process of representing language in writing. As the early literacy experts maintained, spelling words can be a useful route to reading as we can always read words we have spelled.

Amazing facts

Research shows that successful spellers need to have developed a number of skills. Before even converting sounds into letters, they have to extract these sounds from the continuous stream of speech into words and then into phonemes. David Crystal's extensive work on the structure and origins of the English language makes the interesting point that spelling requires the ability to form linear sequences of letters, rather than just the visual pattern-recognition required in reading whole words.

The previous belief that spelling was principally a visual skill was evidenced by the use of the 'look-cover-write-check' strategy. In fact it requires both a visual skill in recalling the correct representation from a range of phonemically plausible versions, and phonic knowledge, as even experienced writers need knowledge of phonics to spell unfamiliar words.

Teaching ideas

● Work on blending should be closely linked to segmenting. This is helped by the use of the following strategies within each phonics session:
  - Hear it: you say several words that contain the specific phoneme so the children can identify the phoneme.
  - Say it: help children to enunciate the phoneme correctly.
  - Read it: read the graphemes, blending phonemes together to make words.
  - Write it: you say a phoneme and the children write the corresponding grapheme. You could also say a word, then segment it into phonemes and ask the children to write the word.

● One of the most powerful ways of teaching segmentation is through the use of 'robot talk' (see Chapter 3). It is important to provide plenty of practice of this in phonics sessions or at other appropriate times in the day.

● Frequent modelling of the process of orally segmenting words and then writing the corresponding graphemes (on an individual whiteboard, for example) is essential. This could be linked to writing items of particular interest or something significant that has happened to the children, for example *I went to the park*.

● Encourage children to link reading and writing (blending phonemes and segmenting words into phonemes) by making their own books which contain sentences they can read phonetically. Ensure that the sentences are related to children's own experiences or interests, and either scribe them for individual children or encourage children to write their own sentences.

● The use of 'phoneme fingers' and also sound buttons can support children in counting phonemes accurately. Both of these are very useful for teaching children to segment words into the constituent phonemes. This will require frequent practice in most phonic sessions. (For more details see Chapter 3.)

● In shared writing, encourage children to suggest graphemes as they are written, for example an adult says: *I want to write the word 'clap'. Who can tell me which phonemes they can hear in 'clap'? Yes, good, /c/ /l/ /a/ /p/. How do I write /c/? What comes next?*

● Provide practice at segmenting words and writing the corresponding graphemes, using partner work and individual whiteboards. This can be by reading out words that include phonemes that the children have been taught, or by providing some sentences on the interactive whiteboard that contain a missing word. Ask the children to work out the missing words and write them on their whiteboards with their partner's help, for example:

It is a — day.
Pat the — dog.

● Constant reference to 'robot talk', or the puppet who can only speak in phonemes, will support children in writing words, so that they realise they first need to split the word into phonemes orally and then write corresponding graphemes for each phoneme.

Resources

Brown Bear, Brown Bear, What Do You See? by Bill Martin and Eric Carle (Picture Puffin)

Quick Fix for Phonics by Wendy Jolliffe (Scholastic)

Teaching Systematic Synthetic Phonics in Primary Schools by Wendy Jolliffe and David Waugh with Angela Carss (Sage)

Letters and Sounds: Principles and practice of high quality phonics (DfES, 2007)

National Curriculum for English Key Stages 1 and 2 – Draft (DfE, 2012) *Independent Review of the Teaching of Early Reading, Final Report* by Jim Rose (DfES, 2006)

Criteria for Assuring High-quality Phonic Work (DfE, 2011)

Common exception words

English has a number of irregular and yet common words that children will need to know very early on when learning to read. While most of these can be decoded once all the phonic rules are learned, children need to be able to read these words before they are able to acquire full decoding skills. These irregular words are known as 'common exception' or 'high-frequency' words.

In the past the emphasis was placed on learning common exception words by sight and this is still necessary to a certain extent. It is useful for children to be able to read these common words quickly so as to speed up their ability to decode texts – this is particularly important as these irregular words make up a high proportion of written English. Many programmes recommend learning about 100 words as high-frequency/ sight words. *Letters and Sounds* (DCSF, 2007) provides a list of 100 words in Appendix 1. However, in order that children do not begin to rely on whole-word recognition as a reading strategy, it is best to limit the number of sight words children learn. In addition, research has shown that demonstrating the grapheme/phoneme correspondences (GPCs) of parts of irregular words is also helpful. There therefore needs to be a programme of a limited number of common exception words (approximately 40) that should be taught in a clear progression, alongside a systematic phonics programme.

Irregular words in English

Subject facts

The English language has absorbed many influences in its development and this has created some irregularities, as discussed in Chapter 4. Nevertheless, about 85% of English is regular, where phonics is a useful key to unlocking the alphabetic code. There are three main historical sources for English spelling patterns:

- Germanic – from the Anglo Saxons; over half of our words fall into this category
- Romance – Latin, French and, in the 16th century, Spanish and Portuguese
- Greek – the language of areas of knowledge (such as physics and philosophy)

Many common words, such as *was*, originate from Old English, while other words reflect Norman influence, particularly the introduction of 'gh' instead of 'h' in words such as *night*, and 'ch' instead of 'c' in words such as *church*. These varied influences, and the resulting irregularities of form, have led to a reluctance to use phonics when teaching reading and spelling in English. The following extract from a Victorian sage expresses the confusion that can be caused:

Dearest creature in creation,
Studying English pronunciation,
I will teach you in my verse
Sounds like corpse, corps, horse
And worse.
It will keep you, Susy, busy,
Make your head with heat grow
Dizzy;
Tear in eye your dress you'll tear.
So shall I! Oh, hear my prayer.

From 'The Chaos'
by Gerard Nolst Trenité, 1922

Recognising GPCs in common exception words

While common exception words are tricky to decode, many of
these words contain parts which are regular and are therefore
phonically decodeable. Although some contain unusual GPCs,
the regular parts offer a good starting point to teach them from,
especially once the children have learnt long-vowel sounds.

The draft National Curriculum emphasises that while
the order of teaching common exception words may vary,
an understanding of the grapheme/phoneme correspondences
(GPCs) in each word is still important:

> *The number, order and choice of exception words taught will
> vary according to the phonics programme being used. Ensuring
> that pupils are aware of the GPCs they contain, however unusual
> these are, supports spelling later.*

Which words?

Rather than the 100 or more words provided in some
programmes and contained in *Letters and Sounds*, there are only
about 40 that need to be taught as whole words, to be read
on sight. These consist of the following, which are arranged in
a sequence for possible teaching and grouped by similarity:

the, to, I, no, go, into
he, she, we, me, be
was, my, you, her, they
all, are, some, come, said
like, do, so, were, when
have, their, out, little, two
what, once, one, because, your
what, where, there, who, people

Why you need to know these facts

● Understanding the origins of the irregularity of the English
spelling system can help explain the seemingly random nature

of spelling. In spite of this, there are a large number of common spelling patterns and these are supported by learning phonics.

● It is important to encourage children to use phonic knowledge even with common exception words where it may only apply to parts of the word. Research has shown that even recognising words by sight is more efficient when underpinned by knowledge of GPCs.

Amazing facts

One way to support the learning of English spelling has been to learn spelling rules. However, even the most common – 'i' before 'e' except after 'c' – has many exceptions, and some scholars consider it to be of no help. Diane McGuinness (see Resources) maintains that rules have exceptions and are therefore not worth teaching (although she does feel that the rule about which letters form digraphs – such as 'sh' in *ship* – is useful). However, there are some rules which work in a majority of cases and are useful for children, for example adding '-es' to the end of words that end in '-s' to make the plural, such as *bus* and *buses*.

Handy tip

The use of mnemonics, or sayings, can be helpful in supporting children learning tricky words, for example:

> said – **S**ally **A**nn **i**s **d**izzy
> because – **b**ig **e**lephants **c**an **a**lways **u**se **s**mall **e**xits.

Mnemonics for parts of the word can also be useful, for example:

> could, would or should – **O U** lucky **d**uck.

Vocabulary

Mnemonic – a device, procedure, or operation that is used to improve memory. For example, to help distinguish *here* and *hear* remember: *You HEAR with your EAR.*

Teaching ideas

● A clear order for teaching common exception words is provided in most phonics programmes, including *Letters and Sounds* where words are grouped within each phonics teaching phase. A teaching sequence is provided below:

1. Make a set of word cards showing a selection of common exception words. It is useful to put these on red card.
2. Display a word card and say it is a *red* word and is difficult to sound out.
3. Point to the word and ask what sound the word begins with and then focus on the tricky part of the word, for example with the word *no*, the 'o' is pronounced as the long /oa/ sound.
4. Underneath the word, put sound buttons (dots) in a different colour, denoting each sound in the word.
5. Group together words with similar sounds, such as *no*, *go* and *so*.
6. Display short sentences or captions containing the word, for example 'Go pat a cat'.
7. Read the caption together.
8. Ask the child to read the caption.
9. Now ask the child to write the word.
10. Display the word and revisit frequently so that the child can read the word straight away.
11. Provide practice in reading such words together with phonically regular words. This combination can be found in many phonics programmes.

Common exception words

● Other useful strategies include clearly differentiating words that are often muddled. Two words which are often confused are *saw* and *was*. In this case it is helpful to clearly point out to children the differences in the words, such as the letter each starts with.

● Playing a variety of games which involve common exception words can be a useful way of engaging children in practising and recalling these words. Some examples include:

- Challenge children to see how many known tricky words they can put in a sentence.
- Print common exception words on cards with duplicates of each for children to play pairs or matching games. Children could also use these cards in a grouping game where they put the words into different categories, for example 'begin with the same letter' and so on.
- Provide children with plastic letters. Display a common exception word, perhaps on an interactive whiteboard, and then delete it. Ask the children to use their letters to make the word from memory.
- Provide a range of words on cards and ask children to make a sentence from a card selected at random.
- Make a large floor chart with examples of common exception words printed on it and play a game similar to 'Twister' where children have to place a hand or foot on the word that you call out.
- Ask a child to select a common exception word, perhaps from a set of cards as suggested above. Keeping the word hidden, they give clues for others to guess which it is, for example: *I have four letters and it means someone has been talking.*
- Play 'Find a word' in a given extract of text, asking children to highlight the chosen word.
- Play dominoes with cards showing common exception words – the last letter of one word should match the first letter of another.
- Play 'Chinese whispers' with a group of children sitting in a circle, where children have to pick up a card with a word printed on it and then whisper it to the person next to them.
- Circle smaller words within words, for example 'he' in *they* and 'one' in *once*.

- Play 'Stepping stones', where children stand on cards with the words printed on them and read the word as they move to the next one, being careful not to fall off into the imagined crocodiles.
- Practise rapid reading of decodable common exception words, using a timer.
- Use a prepared, fully decodable caption that includes common exception words.
- Give pairs of children sets of words containing a particular phoneme. Ask them to take turns, with one child saying a word and the other writing it; they should then check their spellings. The following words, some of which are common exception words, could be used:

/ai/	made, make, away, take, play, day, came, name, they, great, baby, paper, again
/ee/	me, he, she, we, be, been, being, see, seen, tree, people, these
/igh/	I, my, by, why, like, time, night, five, nine, nineteen
/oa/	so, no, go, going, home, old, told, over, open, only, both
/(y)oo/	blue, true, glue.

Resources

Quick Fix for Phonics by Wendy Jolliffe (Scholastic)
Early Reading Instruction: What Science Really Tells Us About How to Teach Reading by Diane McGuinness (Bradford Books)

A systematic progression for phonics

A systematic progression for phonics consists of a structured teaching programme that ensures all 44 phonemes and their major spellings are taught in a clear sequence. Without this systematic approach, children are unable to fully access the alphabetic code. It also needs to be taught quickly and early, and, as stated in Chapter 5, applied frequently in reading and writing.

There is an increasing recognition from governments worldwide of the need to ensure that phonics is taught systematically. This has been backed up by government reports: in the US the report of the National Reading Panel, in the UK the Rose Report, and in Australia the *National Enquiry into the Teaching of Literacy*. In England, this has culminated in a statutory requirement within the draft new National Curriculum for 2014, which emphasises that a rigorous and systematic phonics programme is the best way to ensure that children are able to decode and spell.

There is a range of research evidence to show that such a systematic progression has a real impact on children's emerging literacy skills. Research in 2006 found that systematic phonics teaching:

> ...enables children to make better progress in reading accuracy than unsystematic or no phonics, and that this is true for both normally developing children and those at risk of failure.

Government requirements

Subject facts

The Rose Report, *The Independent Review of the Teaching of Early Reading*, set out clearly what constitutes high-quality phonic work, stating that it should be:

> ...systematic, that is to say, it follows a carefully planned programme with fidelity, reinforcing and building on previous learning to secure children's progress.

The UK Government has also produced criteria for ensuring high-quality phonic programmes, which should:

> ...be designed for the teaching of discrete, daily sessions progressing from simple to more complex phonic knowledge and skills and covering the major grapheme/phoneme correspondences.

The DfE publication *Teachers' Standards* (2012) also states that teachers should demonstrate good subject and curriculum knowledge, and specifically:

> ...if teaching early reading, demonstrate a clear understanding of systematic synthetic phonics.

Why you need to know these facts

● There is a clear Government imperative to ensure that the teaching of systematic synthetic phonics is incorporated in the teaching of early reading. Research also shows that where this is systematic and includes the teaching of all 44 phonemes and their major grapheme correspondences, it is more effective.

Common misconceptions

The Rose Report made it explicit that there should be 'fidelity to the programme'. This has created some confusion in the intervening period and a commonly held interpretation is that teaching should be restricted to one phonics programme, as long as that programme meets the criteria for high-quality phonics work. However, the term refers to fidelity to a framework or structure that therefore ensures that all of the 44-plus phonemes and their alternative spellings and pronunciations are taught and applied in reading and writing. It does not suggest teachers should be restricted to the use of one particular programme.

What are the key features of a systematic progression?

Subject facts

A systematic structured progression for teaching synthetic phonics, as provided by the DfE criteria for phonics programmes, has the following features:

- All 40-plus grapheme/phoneme correspondences (GPCs) are taught in a clear sequence.
- The pace of instruction ensures GPCs are introduced at the rate of about three to five a week, starting with single letters and a sound for each, then going on to the sounds represented by digraphs (for example /sh/ and /oo/) and larger grapheme units (such as /air/ and /igh/).
- Explicit teaching of blending of phonemes for reading is included, starting after the first few GPCs are taught and continued as more GPCs are taught.
- Explicit segmenting of phonemes for spelling is provided, again starting after the first few GPCs are taught and working with more GPCs as more are taught.

- The most common spellings for phonemes are introduced first, followed by the alternative sounds for spellings and the alternative spellings for sounds.
- Strategies are introduced for reading and spelling common exception words containing unusual GPCs.

Ofsted found these features were strongly in evidence in successful schools, and the report *Reading by Six* found that:

> *The diligent, concentrated and systematic teaching of phonics is central to the success of all the schools that achieve high reading standards in Key Stage 1. This requires high-quality and expert teaching that follows a carefully planned and tightly structured approach to teaching phonic knowledge and skills.*

The following is an example cited by Ofsted in its report of one school's approach:

> *Trenance Infant School, Cornwall*
> *The school serves the tourist town of Newquay. The vast majority of the pupils are White British; languages other than English include Polish and Filipino. The current headteacher, Lisa Mannall, took up her post in September 2007, inheriting the structured Read Write Inc. programme for reading and writing that her predecessor had recently adopted.*
>
> *The keys to the school's success were reiterated constantly: absolute consistency across the school; high-quality training and staff development for everyone involved in teaching reading; very strong, logical progression from individual sounds to blending sounds to make words, then sentences, and then reading whole books; setting by attainment, with fluid movement across groups and, every eight weeks, assessment of the progress of each child across the whole school to refine the groupings. In addition, the high-quality, consistent teaching has had a substantial impact on eliminating behavioural problems because the pupils are so engaged.*
>
> Reading by Six (Ofsted, 2010)

- It is necessary to have a thorough understanding of what constitutes a systematic progression for teaching phonics. This then supports daily systematic teaching alongside rigorous assessment. It is vital to know what GPCs should be taught and in what order, and how to do this in lively multi-sensory ways to ensure all children are engaged.

Teaching ideas

- In order to ensure a systematic progression for phonics, teachers should make sure that:
  - a clear framework is used, either based on a phonics programme, or devised by the school, which includes all the features described previously in 'Subject facts'
  - lessons are carefully planned to ensure opportunities for over-learning of phonemes taught
  - there is a fast pace of teaching so that all 44 phonemes and their most common grapheme representations are taught by the end of Year 1
  - children's progress is carefully tracked
  - additional intervention is provided for children who require reinforcement
  - each phonics lesson is structured around four elements: revisit and review, teach, practise, and apply, as recommended by the *Letters and Sounds* programme.

Progression and pace

Subject facts

There is a clear need for a fast-paced teaching programme in order for children to be able to apply their skills in reading and writing. Phonics teaching in the past used to commonly consist of 'a sound a week' which meant that it took almost a school year to learn 26 letter sounds. A prolonged pace of teaching means that children begin to use other strategies such as whole-word recognition to read, rather than applying their phonic skills to decode words. This can later result in children's progress being limited, particularly as they begin to read a wider range of texts. It will also impact on their spelling ability. Without a thorough and automatic use of phonics for reading and writing, children may struggle with reading and spelling unfamiliar words, which in turn will have a detrimental effect on their comprehension skills.

The draft National Curriculum provides a clear structure for 'word reading' divided into year groups. It states that in Year 1:

> *Pupils should be taught to:*
> - *respond speedily with the correct sound to graphemes (letters or groups of letters) for all 40-plus phonemes, including, where applicable, alternative sounds for graphemes*
> - *read accurately by blending sounds in unfamiliar words containing GPCs that have been taught*
> - *read words containing taught GPCs and 's', 'es', 'ing', 'ed', 'er' and 'est' endings*
> - *read other words of more than one syllable that contain taught GPCs.*

Why you need to know these facts

● A clear knowledge of progression and pace is a further key aspect in teaching phonics effectively. Knowing why children should learn this fast and what expectations are for children at the age of six, for example, is necessary to ensure that requirements of the national phonics screening test for six-year-olds can be met. More information on this test can be found in Chapter 8.

Teaching ideas

A lesson structure for teaching phonics should provide opportunities to revisit previously taught phonemes, explicit teaching of new phonemes and application in reading and writing. The *Letters and Sounds* framework structures lessons as follows:

1. **Revisit and review**
   Practise previously learned grapheme/phoneme correspondences (GPCs).
   Practise oral blending and segmentation of previously learned phonemes.

2. **Teach**
   Teach a new GPC.
   Teach blending and/or segmentation with letters.
   Teach one or two common exception or 'tricky' words.

3. **Practise**
   Practise reading the new GPC and spelling words containing this new GPC.

4. **Apply**
   Read or write a sentence/caption using one or more common exception words and words containing the new GPC.

Reviewing programme structures

Subject facts

Most published phonics programmes provide a clear structure for teaching and, in order to meet the criteria for high-quality phonics work and to receive matched funding from the DfE, they need to ensure that grapheme/phoneme (letter/sound) correspondences (GPCs) are taught in a clearly defined, incremental sequence (the alphabetic principle).

Letters and sounds

Letters and Sounds outlined the progression and pace recommended. This progression is divided into six phases

A systematic progression for phonics

as shown on the following page.

Phase 1
● **Main purpose:** Through speaking and listening activities, children will develop their language structures and increase their vocabulary. In developing their phonological awareness, children will improve their ability to distinguish between sounds and to speak clearly and audibly with confidence and control. They become familiar with rhyme, rhythm and alliteration.

● **Outcome:** Children explore and experiment with sounds and words. They listen attentively. They show a growing awareness and appreciation of rhyme, rhythm and alliteration. They speak clearly and audibly with confidence and control. They distinguish between different sounds in words and begin to develop awareness of the differences between phonemes.

● **Typical duration:** Ongoing.

Phase 2
● **Main purpose:** To introduce GPCs.

● **Outcome:** Children know that words are constructed from phonemes and that phonemes are represented by graphemes. They have knowledge of a small selection of common consonants and vowels. They blend them together in reading simple CVC words and segment them to support spelling.

● **Typical duration:** Up to six weeks.

Phase 3
● **Main purpose:** To teach children one grapheme for each of the 44 phonemes in order to read and spell simple regular words.

● **Outcome:** Children link sounds to letters, naming and sounding the letters of the alphabet. They recognise letter shapes and say a sound for each. They hear and say sounds in the order in which they occur in the word, and read simple words by sounding out and blending the phonemes all through the word from left to right. They recognise common digraphs and read some high-frequency words.

- **Typical duration:** Up to 12 weeks.

Phase 4
- **Main purpose:** To teach children to read and spell words containing adjacent consonants.

- **Outcome:** Children are able to blend and segment adjacent consonants in words and to apply this skill when reading unfamiliar texts and in spelling.

- **Typical duration:** Four to six weeks.

Phase 5
- **Main purpose:** To teach children to recognise and use alternative ways of pronouncing the graphemes and spelling the phonemes already taught.

- **Outcome:** Children will use alternative ways of pronouncing the graphemes and spelling the phonemes corresponding to long-vowel phonemes. Children will identify the constituent parts of two-syllable and three-syllable words and be able to read and spell phonically decodable two-syllable and three-syllable words. They will recognise an increasing number of high-frequency words automatically. Phonic knowledge and skills will be applied as the prime approach in reading and spelling when the words are unfamiliar and not completely decodable.

- **Typical duration:** Securing reading and spelling will extend through Year 1.

Phase 6
- **Main purpose:** To teach children to develop their skill and automaticity in reading and spelling, creating ever-increasing capacity to discern meaning from reading.

- **Outcome:** Children apply their phonic skills and knowledge to recognise and spell an increasing number of complex words. They read an increasing number of high- and medium-frequency words independently and automatically.

- **Typical duration:** For the majority of children this phase will begin in and continue through Year 2 so that by the end this year they should be well on the way to becoming fluent readers.

Other programmes

Other systematic phonics programmes follow a similar progression. *Jolly Phonics*, for example, has seven steps and then a 'further phonics' stage which introduces less common spellings for long-vowel sounds. A downloadable summary of these steps for teaching reading and writing with *Jolly Phonics* can be accessed from the resources section of www.jollylearning.co.uk

Read Write Inc.

This programme includes the following progression:
- **Phase 1:** Rhyme, rhythm, vocabulary development.
- **Phase 2:** Approximately 24 GPCs
- **Phase 3:** 18 more GPCs
- **Phase 4:** Adjacent consonants
- **Phase 5:** Alternative GPCs
- **Phase 6:** Automaticity of above

Quick Fix for Phonics

This programme from Scholastic aims to support children who have not made expected progress in learning phonics. It is divided into the following steps:
- **Step 1:** Diagnostic assessment of children's phonic knowledge
  A range of activities designed to accurately assess children's phonic knowledge from the start.
- **Step 2:** Revisiting consonants and short vowels
  A series of detailed multi-sensory lesson plans to support any phonemes that may not be secure.
- **Step 3:** Revisiting long-vowel sounds
  The focus here is on supporting children's understanding of the more complex long-vowel sounds and their alternative spellings using a range of engaging methods.

The programme teaches all the 44 GPCs, as set out in the following charts:

Consonant phonemes and short-vowel phonemes			
Phoneme	**Common spellings**	**Phoneme**	**Common spellings**
/s/	sun, mouse, city, mess, science, mice	/f/	fish, photo, coffee
/a/	apple	/l/	leg, spell
/t/	tap, better	/h/	hat
/p/	paper, hippo	/sh/	ship, mission, chef
/i/	ink, bucket	/z/	zebra, please, is, fizzy, sneeze
/n/	noise, knife, gnat	/w/	water, wheel, queen
/e/	egg, bread	/ch/	chip, watch
/d/	dog, puddle	/j/	jug, judge, giant, barge
/m/	man, hammer, comb	/v/	van, drive
/g/	game, egg	/y/	yes
/o/	octopus, want	/th/	thin
/c/ /k/	luck, cat, Chris, king, queen	/th/	then
/u/	umbrella, love	/ng/	ring, sink
/r/	rabbit, wrong, berry	/zh/	treasure
/b/	baby, cabbage		

A systematic progression for phonics

Long-vowel phonemes

Phoneme	Common spellings	Phoneme	Common spellings
/ai/	play, take, snail, baby	/ur/	burn, girl, term, heard, work
/ee/	feel, heat, me, pony	/or/	sauce, horn, door, warn, claw, ball
/igh/	tie, fight, my, bike, tiger	/ar/	car
/oa/	float, slow, stone, nose	/air/	hair, bear, share
/oo/	book, could, put	/ear/	ear, here, deer
/oo/	moon, clue, grew, tune	/ure/	sure, tour
/ow/	cow, shout	/ə/	teacher, collar, doctor, wooden, circus
/oi/	coin, boy		

Why you need to know these facts

● It is important to be aware of the different phonics programmes available and to understand the structure, pace and benefits of any programmes you use, so that you can deliver them effectively. A systematic progression in teaching synthetic phonics should have the following features:

- It begins with learning grapheme/phoneme correspondences (GPCs) starting with some consonants and short vowels (commonly 's', 'a', 't', 'p', 'i' and 'n') in order for children to be able to blend these into CVC words from the outset.
- A greater number of GPCs are then taught including long-vowel sounds. Different programmes may do this in a

different order, but the 40-plus phonemes are introduced systematically.

- A small number of common exception words that are complex to decode are introduced and taught (commonly three to five per week).
- Alternative pronunciations and spellings for graphemes are then taught.
- The application of GPCs taught in reading and writing is provided throughout.

Vocabulary

Adjacent consonants – consonants that appear next to each other in a word and that can be blended together for example 'bl' in *blip* and 'cr' in *crisp*.

Teaching ideas

Teaching phonics in a systematic progression requires the teacher to consider three main aspects:

1. Ensure the ongoing development of children's phonological awareness.
2. Teach all GPCs in a clear sequence, alongside some common exception words.
3. Provide opportunities for regular assessment of children's progress, with additional support as required.

These requirements are explained in more detail on the following page:

1. Teaching phonological awareness

Teaching phonological awareness is included in Phase 1 of *Letters and Sounds* and it is discussed at length in Chapter 2 of this book. This includes developing:

- listening skills
- awareness of, and ability to manipulate, rhymes
- the ability to discriminate syllables

- the ability to discriminate phonemes.

In effect, teaching progresses from considering larger units of sound to smaller units, as children's discriminating skills develop. However, as discussed in Chapter 2, it does not require a lengthy period of teaching for most children, as this skill can be developed alongside the systematic teaching of phonemes.

2. Teaching the GPCs
Step 1

The first step in teaching the GPCs in a clear sequence starts with teaching consonants and short-vowel sounds, which then enables children to blend these phonemes into words. This is an important step in encouraging them to apply their phonic knowledge. A typical lesson at this stage would include the following:

- **Hear it:** Say a range of words containing the phoneme in the initial position and then ask children to identify the phoneme. Reinforce with an alliterative phrase and an appropriate action.

- **Say it:** Reinforce correct pronunciation of the sound and ask children to practise saying it several times. Use 'robot talk' (see Chapter 3), saying several words containing the phoneme taught and ask the children to blend the phonemes into words.

- **Read it:** Show a card with the grapheme on and say the phoneme. Combine with other phonemes taught to blend as soon as possible.

- **Write it:** Say the phoneme again and ask the children to write the letter. Provide cues for letter formation and apply the letter to whole words as soon as possible.

Step 2

The next step is to teach a greater number of GPCs, in addition to introducing digraphs, and to gradually teach some common exception words. For comprehensive guidance on teaching these words, see Chapter 6. A typical lesson at this stage would include:

- **Review:** Here children should be encouraged to practise hearing, saying, reading and writing phonemes taught. Use phoneme cards containing the letter(s) representing the phonemes and an illustration to review phonemes taught. Reinforce by saying several words containing these phonemes using 'robot talk', for example /w/ /i/ /sh/ and /b/ /u/ /zz/. Ask the children to blend the phonemes into words and tell a partner. Children can also be encouraged to use 'robot talk' themselves and to say words in phonemes, practising their ability to segment words. It is useful to display the phonemes taught so far (for example *wag, zip* and *shop*) for the children to see and read, and then to practise writing. Opportunities for them to write similar words using individual whiteboards should also be provided.

- **Teach:** Teach a new phoneme by introducing a phoneme card and providing plenty of opportunities for children to say the sound; an alliterative phrase is helpful, so for example with /ch/, the phrase could be *Chop chips and cheese*. With young children, the use of actions also helps to encourage multi-sensory learning. After children have practised saying the sound, and their enunciation has been checked, they should be encouraged to read the corresponding letters (grapheme) – for example 'ch'. When introducing a digraph, explain that this sound is written with two letters and use the term 'digraph'. Even young children soon learn the correct terminology.

- **Practise:** Here the children should have opportunities to read and write words containing the new phoneme, for example for /ch/: *chick, chop, chip* and so on. Correct letter formation should be reinforced: this may include demonstration using fingers in the air, then modelling formation using a pen and whiteboard, before the children practise themselves.

- **Apply:** Writing sentences for the children to read and encouraging them to write their own sentences provides valuable practice in applying phonemes. It is also helpful to use decodable texts, which are available to accompany many phonics programmes.

Step 3

At this stage, teach alternative graphemes for the same phoneme.

● **Revisit and review:** Using the phoneme cards for a number of familiar phonemes, ask the individual child or small group of children, to quickly tell you the phonemes. Make this a race or speed trial to see how quickly they can tell you these phonemes.

● **Teach:** Remind the child of the phoneme, for example /s/, and ask them to write the letter on a whiteboard and show you. Say a word containing the phoneme (such as *sit*) that the child is able to write and then ask them to write it. Explain that there are different ways of spelling sounds, so that in *mess* we spell /s/ with 'ss' and in *city* we spell it with 'c'. You might like to talk about the position of the sound in the word and the difference this makes: for example we are unlikely to start a word with 'ss', but in a word with one syllable, ending in the sound /s/, we often end with 'ss'.

● **Practise:** Provide opportunities to read and write the GPCs. First write some words containing the phoneme (such as *hiss*, *mess*, *fuss*, *kiss*) and then ask the child to read the word, blending the phonemes together. Place 'sound buttons' to denote the phonemes underneath one word and ask the child to do the same with other words. Now say a word containing the phoneme, such as *boss*, and ask the child to write it on their whiteboard.

● **Apply:** With the child, read captions containing the phoneme, for example:

I like cress.
A cross boss.

● **Dictate:** Read out a sentence or two for the child to write, for example:

Press the dress.
I like chess.
Miss Pit gets cross.

Step 4

Teaching the long-vowel phonemes and their alternative GPCs is usually the final stage in teaching phonics. This is the most complex aspect and requires careful multi-sensory teaching. For full guidance on this aspect, see Chapter 4.

3. Providing opportunities for regular assessment

Providing ongoing and tracked assessment of children's progress is a vital part of successful phonics teaching. The different types of assessment are explained in detail in Chapter 8.

Resources

Teaching Reading: Report and Recommendations – National Inquiry into the Teaching of Literacy (Department of Education, Science and Training, Australia, 2005)

Quick Fix for Phonics by Wendy Jolliffe (Scholastic)

Teaching Children to Read: An evidence-based assessment of the scientific research literature on reading and its implications for reading instruction (National Institute of Child Health and Human Development, USA, 2000)

Reading by Six (Ofsted, 2010)

Independent Review of the Teaching of Early Reading – Final Report by Jim Rose (DfES, 2006)

A Systematic Review of the Research Literature on the Use of Phonics in the Teaching of Reading and Spelling by Carole J Torgerson, Greg Brooks and Jill Hall (DfES, 2006)

Criteria for Assuring High-quality Phonic Work (DfE, 2011)

Chapter 8

Assessing phonic skills

One of the most important aspects in teaching phonics is accurate and ongoing assessment of children's progress. The *Criteria for Assuring High-quality Phonic Work* by the DfE states that:

> ...if a programme is high quality, systematic and synthetic it will, by design, map incremental progression in phonic knowledge and skills. It should therefore enable teachers to: track children's progress; assess for further learning and identify incipient difficulties, so that appropriate support can be provided.

The importance of assessment

Subject facts

Assessment should be continuous and planned for to ensure children have sufficiently grasped those aspects taught. Working in this way, it is easy to diagnose any problems. It is then possible to re-teach or consolidate learning by providing specific and alternative activities to address the difficulties. It is important to ensure that progress is carefully tracked. Frequent opportunities must be provided for reviewing the phonemes children have already been taught – it is this process of 'over-learning' that is so crucial for successful phonics acquisition.

Ofsted's survey, *Removing Barriers to Literacy*, specifically found that one of the key factors that makes a positive difference to the outcome of phonics teaching is the decision to:

...teach phonics systematically as part of the teaching of reading and ensure that pupils' progress in developing their phonic knowledge and skills is regularly assessed.

In the Ofsted survey, schools that were successful in teaching phonics demonstrated that:

The assessment of pupils' understanding of letters, sounds and words was frequent and record-keeping was meticulous.

This highlights the importance of making use of regular assessment and tracking data to plan for appropriate and challenging lessons.

Types of assessment

The methods of assessment for phonics, as for any other subject, can be divided into several types. The principal types are 'formative assessment' (or 'assessment for learning') where children are assessed as part of the ongoing teaching, and 'summative assessment' ('assessment *of* learning') where an assessment is made which sums up a child's achievement at a given point in time. Another type of assessment that is particularly useful for phonics is 'diagnostic assessment'.

Why you need to know these facts

● A clear understanding of the different types of assessment, particularly for teaching phonics, underpins effective teaching. Providing ongoing assessment as part of every phonics lesson ensures that children's progress is carefully tracked and that, when required, further reinforcement is provided. At key intervals, such as every half term, children's progress should also be recorded in order to determine whether it meets expectations which will have been clearly set out in advance (see *Letters and Sounds* for examples). For children who are causing concern, a diagnostic assessment may be required to identify particular difficulties (Scholastic's *Quick Fix for Phonics* provides examples of diagnostic tests).

Vocabulary

Assessment for learning – defined by the Assessment Reform Group as the process of seeking and interpreting evidence for use by learners and their teachers to decide where the learners are in their learning, where they need to go and how best to get there. (Also known as 'formative assessment'.)

Diagnostic assessment – carried out individually with children to ascertain exactly what the child knows and understands; can identify any gaps in their learning and next steps for teaching.

Formative assessment – the process of obtaining information to decide what stage learners have reached in their learning; crucially informs the next steps using the information gained. (Also known as 'assessment for learning'.)

Summative assessment – assessment *of* learning, designed to measure student achievement and gauge what they have learned.

Tracking – recording each child's progress against the stages or phases of a phonics programme.

Ongoing formative assessment

Subject facts

Inevitably, some children will make slower progress, and this is why assessment for learning, where a teacher carefully provides opportunities in all lessons to check children's progress, is so vital. Many phonics programmes provide guidance on how to include this. The *Letters and Sounds* guidance on assessment and tracking identifies the range of opportunities for assessment:

> This can be during the discrete daily phonics session, but will also be apparent during shared, guided and independent reading and writing sessions. Writing samples provide useful evidence of children's phonic knowledge and ability to apply phonic skills, but evidence obtained through observation of children's approaches to reading unfamiliar words is of equal importance.

It is also important to bear in mind that there is often an overlap between different stages or phases in phonics teaching, as the *Letters and Sounds* 'Notes of Guidance for Practitioners and Teachers' points out:

> In 'Letters and Sounds' the boundaries between the phases are deliberately porous so that no children are held back, or unduly pressured to move on before they are equipped to do so. It follows that practitioners and teachers will need to make principled decisions based on reliable assessments of children's learning to inform planning for progression within and across the phases.

While teachers must ensure that children have grasped particular grapheme/phoneme correspondences (GPCs), it is also crucial that children are not held back if they are ready to progress. This is why most phonics programmes contain a 'revisit and review' section in each lesson.

Tracking

Progress in learning phonics is largely hierarchical and, as children are taught a systematic progression, it is important that each child's progress is carefully tracked. Many phonics schemes, such as *Letters and Sounds*, provide a phonics progress tracking sheet to map children's progress.

It is essential to distinguish on such tracking sheets the difference between children who are working at a particular phase and those children who are secure at a phase. Children are judged to be secure at a particular phase once they consistently know most of the phonemes associated with that phase, and can apply the skills of blending and segmenting using an appropriate range of GPCs. Teachers need to develop systems, such as highlighting children's names or initials, to denote when they are secure at a particular phase.

Why you need to know these facts

● Regular assessment of children's developing phonic knowledge and skills is one of the key elements of effective phonics teaching. At each stage, if progress information is obtained, teachers can adjust their planning to fit the needs of their students. For example, early assessment for learning can establish whether children have developed good phonological awareness before they begin learning phonics. Understanding how ongoing assessment informs successful phonics teaching helps ensure that assessment is planned for and included in every phonics lesson.

Teaching ideas

● To assess phoneme discrimination, ask individual children to listen to the word you say and then tell you the sound they hear at the beginning, middle or end of the word. Choose simple monosyllabic words and ensure correct enunciation of the sounds.

● To assess blending skills for reading, display a range of nonsense words to reflect a child's phonic knowledge, and ask them to read the words (for example *bec, sal, fet, mig*). Children need to know these are not real words and they may like to make up further words themselves.

● To assess children's segmenting skills, provide each child or pair with an individual whiteboard and pen, and carry out the following steps:
  • Say a word containing the phoneme being taught and other learned phonemes (for example for /t/, the word *tap*). Ask the children to repeat the word.
  • Now ask the children to split the word (segment it) into phonemes (for example /t/ /a/ /p/). They should say each phoneme, counting on their fingers the corresponding number.
  • They then hold up their fingers to show you how many phonemes (for example three for *tap*).
  • Ask them to write the word on their whiteboards and then show you.

● Phoneme fingers: This activity is used to check children's ability to segment words into phonemes. Here the teacher says a word, for example *crash*, and then asks the children to work out how many phonemes it contains. Then the teacher says *3-2-1 and show me!* The children hold up the corresponding number of fingers for phonemes (in this case, four).

Summative assessment

Subject facts

Summative assessment may be carried out at certain key points to record progress, for example at the end of a school term or year. There are some commercial tests that allow teachers to conduct these with larger groups (for example *Fast Phonics First*, see Resources). These principally consist of sentences where a word is missing and the child selects the appropriate word by putting a circle around it. For example:

> The dog ran in the… *(road, rode)*.

Assessment should include the following stages:
- Read and spell grapheme/phoneme correspondences (GPCs) taught. This should be broken down into stages, such as starting with the first GPCs (/s/, /a/, /t/, /p/, /i/ and /n/).
- Read and spell CVC words.
- Read and spell words containing consonant clusters (for example *scrap, flip* and *crack*).
- Read and spell words containing split digraphs.
- Read and spell words containing long-vowel digraphs.

Why you need to know these facts

- As phonics is taught systematically in stages, it is important to assess whether children have reached these stages and to summarise their progress at regular intervals.

Teaching ideas

The following ideas for conducting summative assessments will support effective recording of progress:

● Ask children to read a decodable text at their phonic level and score them according to each word they read correctly.

● Invite children to spell a range of words within their expected phonic level and record their scores.

● Provide children with a range of nonsense words at their expected level and score them as they read. For a range of these, including CVC words, words containing adjacent consonants, and words with long-vowel digraphs, see the tables at the end of this chapter.

Diagnostic assessment

Subject facts

Where teachers have not been able to gather sufficient information from observations to provide a clear picture of children's achievements, or where they have concerns about a particular child, a more focused adult-led assessment should be undertaken. This will inform the teaching programme required.

Phonics screening check for six-year-olds

One example of a check which can be used for diagnostic purposes is the phonics screening programme that was introduced for all Year 1 children in 2012, which gives clear indications of the expectations of children's phonic ability by the end of Year 1. As the Ofsted report *Reading By Six* explains, the screening check framework provides the following statements to indicate additional skills that children should have by the end of Year 1:

Children should be able to:
- *apply phonic knowledge and skill as the prime approach to reading unfamiliar words that are not completely decodable*
- *read many frequently encountered words automatically*
- *read phonically decodable three-syllable words*
- *read a range of age-appropriate texts fluently*
- *demonstrate understanding of age-appropriate texts.*

In terms of phonics specifically, the screening check framework says that children are expected to:

- *give the sound when shown any grapheme that has been taught*
- *blend phonemes in order to read words*
- *know most of the common grapheme–phoneme correspondences*
- *read phonically decodable one-syllable and two-syllable words.*

The screening check contains 40 words divided into two sections of 20 words. Both sections contain a mixture of real words and non-words ('nonsense' words). All non-words in the screening check are accompanied by a picture of an imaginary creature to provide a context for the child (naming the type of imaginary creature) to ensure that they are not trying to match the non-word to a word in their vocabulary. The screening process will give clear and concise information about a child's phonic ability at a young age, allowing any necessary intervention to begin at an early stage.

Why you need to know these facts

- It is important to have a clear understanding of the range of areas of a child's phonic knowledge that need to be assessed in order to diagnose specific difficulties. It is also necessary to recognise the useful role that nonsense words, or non-words, play in enabling the assessment of blending skills.

One misconception concerns the use of non-words or nonsense words. Some critics believe that only real words should be taught and that being exposed to nonsense words will only ultimately confuse children. In fact, if you clearly state that these are nonsense words, their use helps children to master the process of sounding and blending phonemes and to demonstrate their abilities. However, this activity should not detract from the principal reading aim of reading for meaning, and therefore needs to be introduced carefully. It is used in the DfE phonics check for six-year-olds which commenced in summer 2012. As the guidance shows, the use of non-words, or nonsense words, is useful in identifying children's ability to use phonic decoding, as long as efforts are made to distinguish such words from real words.

Teaching ideas

Individual diagnostic assessments will need to cover a range of aspects including:

Graphemes and phonemes
● Provide children with a list of graphemes that they have been taught (not in alphabetical order) and ask them to tell you the sounds they make.

● Read out some letters and appropriate words from taught phonemes for children to write.

Assessing blending skills
● Start by clearly stating that you are going to read some nonsense words, and demonstrate by reading some. Then provide children with a list of nonsense words made up of only phonemes they have been taught (see the end of this chapter for examples) and ask them to read the list, assessing how they blend the phonemes in each case.

Assessing segmenting skills

● Pronounce a word and ask the child to repeat it. Then ask them to tell you the sounds from first to last (alternatively, they could use 'phoneme fingers', as described above).

● Provide magnetic or plastic letters for children to use. Pronounce a word and ask the child to repeat it before they select the appropriate letters to make the word.

● Pronounce a word and ask the child to repeat it before they write the word.

Intervention and support

Subject facts

Assessing and tracking children's progress is necessary in order to support those children who may not have fully grasped some phonemes and the corresponding graphemes.

It is wise to consider carefully before withdrawing children from whole-class phonics teaching if they seem to be progressing at a slower pace. Children who are having difficulties benefit from the whole-class experience of blending and segmenting and from hearing a range of phonemes, in addition to being exposed to wider vocabulary. Further support may be provided individually or in small groups as necessary to supplement this.

When undertaking any intervention programme, it is first important to base this on accurate assessment of a child's needs. It is also essential that the children recognise that the goal of all phonics lessons is to achieve fluent word recognition and effortless reading and writing. There is a need, therefore, to continually apply the learning to reading using decodable texts and to include frequent opportunities to write.

Effective intervention can often be carried out by teaching those children identified as needing additional support in small groups. It is important that the children in these groups are of a similar ability in order to provide the most suitable support for each individual. Planning for these individuals or groups should be carried out by the class teacher as part of the wider class planning for phonics, in order to promote consistency and a systematic approach. It is also crucial that the adults who lead any intervention groups maintain records and provide feedback to the class teacher to inform future planning and target setting.

Why you need to know these facts

● Accurate assessment is essential for identifying children who need additional support and research shows that effective early intervention can prevent later literacy problems. The heart of good phonics teaching therefore lies in good assessment procedures.

Teaching ideas

When providing support for those children identified as progressing at a slower pace, various grouping arrangements may be helpful.

● In order to ensure that children do not miss out on the benefits of whole-class teaching, you could provide additional lessons in small groups. These could be before the main lesson to prepare children or afterwards to help them catch up, and may be taken by the class teacher or a teaching assistant.

● Some children will benefit from one-to-one work with a trained teaching assistant.

● A child or a small group of children could be supported within a lesson by a teaching assistant.

● A group of children who are at the same level in reading or phase in phonics could be taught together so that the teaching can focus closely on their needs. This could be arranged across several classes in Key Stage 1. If trained teaching assistants are also involved in this teaching time, then those children below target or requiring intervention could be taught in even smaller groups. Especially in Reception, a mixed-ability class could be divided towards the latter part of the academic year for phonic work, to enable the younger or less confident children to make good progress before Year 1.

Supporting older children

Subject facts

Some children at Key Stage 2 may be experiencing difficulty in reading and/or writing because they have missed or misunderstood a crucial phase of systematic phonics teaching. There are a range of 'catch-up' programmes available including *Quick Fix for Phonics* (Scholastic) which is adaptable for Key Stage 2 and includes the following steps, together with detailed lesson plans:

- Step 1: Diagnostic assessment of children's phonic knowledge
- Step 2: Revisiting consonants and short vowels
- Step 3: Revisiting long-vowel sounds

Letters and Sounds intervention programme

Another intervention programme, based on and linked to *Letters and Sounds* (DCSF, 2007), is aimed at Key Stage 2 children who demonstrate difficulties in reading and writing. The materials are designed to guide teachers and suitably trained teaching assistants in supporting children who may have poorly developed phonic knowledge, skills and understanding. As the programme states:

For some children, the missing piece of the jigsaw may be specific items of knowledge that require only a few weeks of short, focused sessions. However, other children may not have crucial concepts such as blending and segmenting in place. Some may have a combination of the two and will require a term or more of consolidation. It is crucial, therefore, that the children's current knowledge is accurately assessed and the gaps identified so that support can be precisely targeted.

The *Letters and Sounds* intervention programme consists of the following steps:

- Step 1: Assess current knowledge from a bank of assessment materials
- Step 2: Identify the need and select the appropriate unit (see overview of units 2, 3, 4 and 5 below)
- Step 3: Teach during regular, short, focused sessions
- Step 4: Assess and then prioritise the next section to teach.

The programme consists of a series of units as follows:

- Unit 1 – assessment
- Unit 2 – linked to Phase 2 *Letters and Sounds*: Grapheme/ phoneme correspondences (GPCs), blending and segmenting; knowledge of the alphabet and letter names
- Unit 3 – linked to Phase 3 *Letters and Sounds*: Consolidation of Phase 2; phonemes consisting of two or more letters (digraphs)
- Unit 4 – linked to Phase 4 *Letters and Sounds*: Consolidation of Phase 2 and Phase 3 and reading and spelling words containing adjacent consonants and polysyllabic words (*creep*, *bring* and *starlight*)
- Unit 5 – linked to Phase 5 *Letters and Sounds*: Consolidation of Phase 2, Phase 3 and Phase 4; alternative spellings for phonemes (/ai/ as in *day*, *came* and *rain*) and alternative pronunciations for graphemes ('ea' – as in *eat*, *bread* and *great*). As Phase 5 is likely to be the area of greatest need at Key Stage 2, this phase has been broken down into four sections, each including groups of graphemes which are most commonly confused by children at Key Stage 2.

Why you need to know these facts

● Teaching phonics is not limited to Key Stage 1 and many older children may need reinforcement, particularly of the long-vowel phonemes and their alternative a spelling choices. If children are encountering difficulties with literacy in Key Stage 2 or later in Key Stage 3, it is essential to ensure that their understanding of phonics is assessed. Phonics can be taught in ways that will engage older children and give them success, particularly with spelling.

Teaching ideas

- Some of the key principles of supporting phonics learning with older children are as follows:
  - Revisit and revise all known graphemes and the associated phonemes, as well as the letter names.
  - Ensure that phonemes are articulated correctly, and that the children repeatedly say them during the sessions.
  - All sessions should continue the same format of four parts that include: revisit and review, teach, practise and apply.

To support the learning of long-vowel phonemes and the alternative spelling choices, an activity such as 'Best bet' is useful as it helps children to recognise the correct spelling of these sounds. For this activity, children draw columns in their books, headed with focused phonemes (see example below for /ai/). They should try and spot a pattern in their lists: for example, the 'ay' grapheme occurs at the end of words, the most common phoneme involving /n/ is /ain/, the most common phoneme involving /k/ is /ake/.

Common				Rare			
ay	ai	a–e	ea	aigh	eigh	e–e	ey
day	rain	lane	great	straight	eight	fete	they
play	wait	mate					
say	train	bake					
may	pain	snake					

- Play 'Countdown', based on the popular TV programme, where children have to make a word from a given number of letters including a long-vowel phoneme. Using magnetic letters, they should try and create the longest word they can to gain the maximum number of points.

Assessment of phonic stages

Start asking the children to identify graphemes, such as:

s	a	t	p	i
n	e	d	m	g

Use non-words to assess their ability to segment consonant-vowel-consonant (CVC) words and writing graphemes, such as:

tog	nal	tam	mip	gep
hig	kug	jek	lom	sul

Use non-words to assess their ability to read and segment adjacent consonants, such as:

pran	scam	skiff	blat	flig
stod	plut	clem	flup	shog
rab	brem	drot	treg	crub
grik	graf	frin	scrot	frod
norp	lind	leck	gisk	tirk

Use non-words to assess their ability to read and segment split digraphs, such as:

loke	pime	pone	lube	hine
wike	hile	sode	cune	soke

Use non-words to assess their ability to read and segment long-vowel phonemes, such as:

leem	pait	hieb	leat	spay
weaf	vay	reeb	laiv	diep
bie	zow	dight	poat	bie
loon	lue	mew	mout	foom
prue	frew	doud	moy	wook
boin	loid	jow	hode	nute
sloud	tuve	doke	toit	froy
terv	zoor	korb	burl	raud
mauv	harl	tirp	sie	vear
gour	plaw	stear	sook	cleer
moad	mair	sare	plaw	tue

Resources

Criteria for assuring high quality phonic work (DfE, 2012)
Removing Barriers to Literacy (Ofsted, 2011)
Letters and sounds (DfES, 2007)
Fast Phonics First (Rigby, 2007)
Phonics: Assessment and Tracking Guidance (DCSF, 2009)

Pronunciation guide

The charts below show the phonemes of the English language and detailed advice on how to pronounce them. As the most common error is to add an 'uh' sound to phonemes (as in 'r' often pronounced 'ruh'), it is vital to ensure they are pronounced correctly.

Phoneme pronunciation chart

Phoneme	Pronunciation guide for children
/s/	When we say /ssss/ the mouth is slightly open and the tongue is flat behind your teeth. Air comes out between your teeth. You can stretch the sound /s/s/s/s/.
/a/	Open your mouth wide and make a loud sound, as if something is nipping you /a/a/a/a/. You can stretch the sound.
/t/	When you say /t/ your mouth is open and your tongue is behind your teeth. It starts at the top of your mouth and goes down, feel the air come out of your mouth as you do it. Make it a very short sound and whisper it /t/t/t/.
/p/	When you say /p/ your lips touch together quickly. Imagine you are blowing a candle out on a cake and make it a very short sound and whisper it /p/p/p/.
/i/	When you say /i/ your mouth is open a tiny bit. The corners of your mouth pull back. You can stretch the sound /i/i/i/i/.

Appendix

Phoneme	Pronunciation guide for children
/n/	When you say /n/ the tip of your tongue goes behind your top teeth and your tongue does not move. You can stretch the sound /n/n/n/n/.
/e/	When you say /e/ your mouth is open a little and your teeth are apart. It looks like you are smiling.
/d/	When you say /d/ you put the tip of your tongue behind your top teeth and your tongue moves down. It's a bit like /t/ but only a little air comes out of your mouth.
/m/	When you say /m/ your lips are together and it sounds like humming. You can stretch the sound /m/m/m/.
/g/	When you say /g/ you can feel the sound right at the back of your mouth. If you put your fingers on your throat you can feel the sound /g/g/g/.
/o/	When you say /o/, your mouth is open and your chin drops down a little. You can stretch the sound /o/o/o/.
/c/ /k/	When you make the sound /k/ you can feel the sound in the back of your mouth. It sounds a bit like /g/, but when you say /k/ you can feel air coming out from your mouth and whisper it /k/k/k/.
/u/	When you say /u/ your mouth is open just a little. You need to push some air out as you do it /u/u/u/.
/r/	When you make the /r/ sound your tongue lifts up in the back of your mouth. It sounds like a car going fast. You can stretch the sound /r/r/r/.
/b/	When you make this sound your lips go together and pop open when you say /b/. It is like /p/ but no air comes out /b/b/b/.

Phoneme	Pronunciation guide for children
/f/	When you say /f/ your teeth touch your bottom lip. You make the /f/ sound by pushing air between your teeth. You can stretch the sound and whisper it /f/f/f/.
/l/	When you say /l/ your tongue moves to the top of your mouth. It stays there as you make the sound in the back of your mouth. You can stretch the sound /l/l/l/.
/h/	When you make the sound /h/ your mouth is open a little. You push air out of your mouth to whisper it /h/h/h/. You can stretch the sound.
/sh/	When you make the sound /sh/ your teeth are together and you push air out of your mouth. It is the sound you make when you want someone to be quiet. You can stretch the sound /sh/sh/sh/.
/z/	When you make the sound /z/ your teeth are together and your tongue is near the front of your mouth and behind your teeth. You push air through your teeth and it makes a buzzing noise. You can stretch the sound /z/z/z/.
/w/	When you say the sound /w/ your lips are close together in a little circle, then they open up /w/w/w/.
/ch/	When you say /ch/ your lips stick out a little. Your teeth are together at first and then they open up. It sounds like a steam train /ch/ch/ch/.
/j/	When you say the sound /j/ your lips stick out a little. Your tongue is near the top of your mouth and it moves when you open your mouth /j/j/j/.
/v/	When you say /v/ your teeth touch your bottom lip. You make the /v/ sound by pushing air between your teeth. You can stretch the sound /v/v/v/.

Phoneme	Pronunciation guide for children
/y/	When you make the /y/ sound your mouth is open a little and your tongue is near the top of your mouth. Your tongue touches the sides of your teeth. Your mouth is open a little more at the end of the sound /y/y/y/.
/th/	When you make the sound /th/ as in *thin*, you put your tongue between your teeth and stick it out. You push air between your tongue and teeth. You can stretch the sound and whisper it /th/th/th/.
/th/	When you make this sound as in *this* your tongue touches the top of your mouth and it vibrates. You can feel the sound in your throat. You can stretch the sound /th/th/th/.
/ng/	When you make this sound it is like a humming sound at the back of your throat but you make it with your mouth open. You can stretch the sound /ng/ng/ng/.
/k/s/ 'x'	When you say 'x' you are saying two sounds /k/ and /s/. You start with the sound /k/ – you can feel the sound in the back of your mouth, and feel air coming out from your mouth as you whisper it /k/. Next you say /s/ – the mouth is slightly open and the tongue is flat behind your teeth. Air comes out between your teeth.
/k/w/ 'qu'	When you say 'qu' you are saying two sounds, /k/ and /w/. You start with the sound /k/ – you can feel the sound in the back of your mouth, and feel air coming out from your mouth as you whisper it /k/. Next you say /w/ – your lips are close together in a little circle, then they open up.
/zh/	When you make this sound your lips are open in a little circle and you blow air through your mouth. Your mouth opens wider at the end of the sound. /zh/zh/zh/.

Glossary

Adjacent consonants – consonants that appear next to each other in a word and that can be blended together for example 'bl' in *blip* and 'cr' in *crisp*.

Alphabetic code – the system or principle by which letters are used to represent the speech sounds of our language.

Analytic phonics – an approach to the teaching of reading in which the phonemes associated with particular graphemes are not pronounced in isolation. Children identify (analyse) the common phonemes in a set of words that each contain the phonemes under study, for example *could, would, should; can, pan, man*. Analytic phonics for writing similarly relies on inferential learning. This approach is often linked to the use of 'onset' and 'rime'.

Assessment for learning – defined by the Assessment Reform Group as the process of seeking and interpreting evidence for use by learners and their teachers to decide where the learners are in their learning, where they need to go and how best to get there. (Also known as 'formative assessment'.)

Blend – to draw sounds, or phonemes, together to pronounce a word, so /s/ /l/ /i/ /p/ equals *slip*.

Common exception words – words that occur frequently in a language but that are irregular (not easily decodable using phonics), for example *said, their* and *one*.

Consonant cluster – two or more consonants that are commonly found at the beginning of words and that do not have an intervening vowel, for example 'str' in *stream*. These are also termed 'adjacent consonants'.

Consonant digraph – two letters representing a consonant phoneme, for example 'ph' in *graph*, 'wh' in *why* and 'gh' in *laugh*.

CVC word – consonant-vowel-consonant words, for example *pat*, *sip* and *pin*.

Decoding – the act of translating graphemes, or letters, into phonemes, or sounds, in order to read words.

Diagnostic assessment – carried out individually with children to ascertain exactly what the child knows and understands; can identify any gaps in their learning and next steps for teaching.

Digraph – two letters that combine to make a new sound.

Encoding – the act of transcribing units of sound, or phonemes, into graphemes for spelling words.

Formative assessment – the process of obtaining information to decide what stage learners have reached in their learning; crucially informs the next steps using the information gained. (Also known as 'assessment for learning'.)

Graph – one letter that makes one sound.

Grapheme – a written representation of a phoneme, that is, a letter or group of letters representing a sound. There is always the same number of graphemes in a word as phonemes. The alphabet contains only 26 letters but by combining the letters in different combinations we can form all the graphemes that represent the phonemes of English.

Grapheme/phoneme correspondence (GPC) – the relationship between the letters and the sounds they represent.

Language comprehension – the process by which words, sentences and discourse are interpreted.

Mnemonic – a device, procedure, or operation that is used to improve memory. For example, to help distinguish *here* and *hear*: *You HEAR with your EAR.*

Onset – in analytic phonics, this is the first part of a word: the consonant or adjacent consonants at the beginning and before the vowel, for example 'fl-' in *flat*.

Phoneme – the smallest unit of sound in a word that can change its meaning (for example, the difference between the phonemes /b/ and /l/ signals the difference in meaning between the words *bed* and *led*). It is generally accepted that most varieties of spoken English use about 44 phonemes. In alphabetic writing systems (such as English) phonemes are represented by graphemes.

Phonemic awareness – the ability to perceive and manipulate the phonemes in spoken words.

Phonological awareness – the ability to perceive, recall and manipulate sounds.

Quadgraph – four letters which combine to make a new sound.

Rime – in analytic phonics, this is the final part of the word: the vowel sound and any consonant sounds that follow it, for example '-at' in *flat*.

Schwa /ə/ – the most common vowel sound in English, it has multiple spellings and is often described as 'weak' as it occurs in unstressed syllables in words. Examples include the final sound in *teacher* and *collar*.

Segment – to split up a word into its constituent sounds, or phonemes, in order to spell it.

Split digraph – two letters, making one sound, which are split by a consonant letter, for example 'a-e' as in *cake*.

Summative assessment – assessment *of* learning, designed to measure student achievement and gauge what they have learned.

Synthetic phonics – an approach to the teaching of reading in which the phonemes (sounds) associated with particular graphemes (letters) are pronounced in isolation and blended together (synthesised). Synthetic phonics for writing reverses the sequence: children are taught to say the word they wish to write, segment it into its phonemes and say them in turn and write a grapheme for each phoneme in turn to produce the written word.

Tracking – recording each child's progress against the stages or phases of a phonics programme.

Trigraph – three letters that combine to make a new sound.

Unvoiced – a sound that is made without using the vocal chords.

Voiced – a sound that is made using the vocal chords.

Word recognition – the ability to recognise words out of context and to apply phonic rules to this recognition.

Index

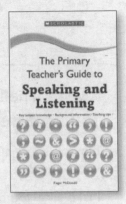